DISCOVERY GUIDE
FIRE ON THE MOUNTAIN

The Faith Lessons™ Series
with Ray Vander Laan

DISCOVERY GUIDE
FIRE ON THE MOUNTAIN

6 FAITH LESSONS™ BY

RAY VANDER LAAN

with Stephen & Amanda Sorenson

ZONDERVAN®   FOCUS ON THE FAMILY®

ZONDERVAN.com/
AUTHORTRACKER
follow your favorite authors

ZONDERVAN

Fire on the Mountain Discovery Guide
Copyright © 2009 by Ray Vander Laan

Requests for information should be addressed to:

Zondervan, *Grand Rapids, Michigan* 49530

Focus on the Family and the accompanying logo and design are federally registered trademarks of Focus on the Family, *Colorado Springs, Colorado* 80995.

That the World May Know and Faith Lessons are trademarks of Focus on the Family.

ISBN 978-0-310-29119-0

All maps created by International Mapping.

All artwork is courtesy of Ray Vander Laan and Mark Tanis.

All illustrations are courtesy of Rob Perry.

Interior design by Ben Fetterley

Printed in the United States of America

10 11 12 13 14 15 16 • 24 23 22 21 20 19 18 17 16 15 14 13 12 11 10 9 8 7 6 5 4 3

CONTENTS

INTRODUCTION

"Let my people go!"

With these simple words, spoken more than 3,200 years ago (Exodus 5:1), God sent Moses to confront the most powerful ruler on earth. By these words, the God of the universe revealed that he had heard the cry of his suffering people. Deeply moved, he revealed himself as the God of love and mercy. He acted with awesome power to deliver the Hebrews and establish them as his chosen instrument to reveal himself to the world.

Few words recorded in the Hebrew Bible, or anywhere for that matter, are more familiar to people today than the words, "Let my people go!" And few events are more central to the stories of both the Hebrew text (Old Testament) and the Christian text (New Testament) than the great redemptive acts of God and the people of the exodus. The Hebrew text refers to the exodus theme more than 120 times, plus there are multiple references to related concepts such as manna, water from the rock, Mount Sinai, and the Ten Commandments. The Christian text mentions Moses eighty-five times and Egypt twenty-nine times.

Yet there is more to the exodus than first meets the eye. The historical account is most useful in understanding God and his desire for the Hebrews to become his witnesses to the world. It is central to understanding why many followers of Jesus considered him to be the prophet like Moses — the Messiah — whom the Lord had promised to send (Deuteronomy 18:17 – 19; Luke 7:16; 24:19 – 20; John 6:14). Jesus often used ideas found in the exodus story, and many of his teachings interpret Moses' words in the Torah. Jesus also positioned his redemptive acts against the background of festivals — Passover, Unleavened Bread, and First Fruits — that are associated with the Hebrews' deliverance from Egypt.[1] And at the deepest level, the exodus story not only provides a background for God's plan to bring Jesus into the world as Messiah, it is one of the first chapters in God's great redemptive story to restore shalom — unity, harmony, order — to his broken creation.

Genesis, the first book of the Torah, provides the necessary background for the exodus. Genesis describes God creating a perfect, harmonious universe out of chaos and then describes how sin destroyed that universe, resulting in the loss of harmony in God's creation and the return of chaos. In the stories of the exodus we find the very foundations of the restoration of shalom to God's world. Future characters in the Scriptures, including Jesus, build on that foundation. To study these amazing events is to discover that there is really one story — the story of God's redemption. Despite the many failures of God's people in fulfilling their role in that story, God's power has and continues to flow through his flawed human instruments (Jesus excepted, of course) to bring to fruition his plan of redemption.

"Let my people go" was the cry of the Hebrews in Egypt. In a sense, it is also the cry of anyone who has recognized the bondage of sin and the destruction it produces. Thus the exodus is a paradigm for our own experience, and we Christians describe our deliverance in similar language because God delivers us by his mercy and the protecting blood of the Lamb — Jesus Christ. Without the exodus, we would not be who we are — redeemed people delivered by the God of Israel. In that sense, the victory of the ancient Hebrews must become our victory. We, like the ancient Hebrews whom God delivered from the hand of Pharaoh, must stand in awe and declare that our God is King.

Clarifying Our Terminology

In this study, the record of God's reclaiming and restoring his broken world is called the Bible, Scripture, or the "text." Having studied in the Jewish world, I believe it is important to communicate clearly how the nature of that inspired book is understood. Although it can be helpful to speak of Scripture in terms of Old and New Testaments, these descriptions also can be misleading if they are interpreted to mean old and outdated in contrast to a new replacement. Nothing, in my opinion, is further from the truth. Whereas the

"New Testament" describes the great advance of God's plan with the arrival of the Messiah and the promise of his completed and continuing work, the "Old Testament" describes the foundational events and people through whom God began that work. The Bible is not complete without both testaments; it comprises God's one revelation, his one plan to reclaim his world and restore harmony between himself and humankind. To emphasize that unity, I prefer to refer to the Hebrew text (Old Testament) and the Christian text (New Testament) that together are the inspired, infallible Word of God.

The language of the Bible is bound by culture and time. The geography of the lands of the Bible — Egypt, the desert, the Promised Land — shaped the people who lived there, and biblical writers assumed that their readers were familiar with the culture of that world. Many Christians today, however, lack even a basic geographical knowledge of the region and know even less of the ancient cultures that flourished there. So understanding the Scriptures involves more than knowing what the words mean. It also means becoming familiar with the everyday experiences and images the text employs to reveal God's message so that we can begin to understand it from the perspective of the people to whom it originally was given.

For example, the ancient Hebrew people to whom God revealed himself described their world in concrete terms. Their language was one of pictures, metaphors, and examples rather than ideas, definitions, and abstractions. Whereas we might describe God as omniscient or omnipresent (knowing everything and present everywhere), they would describe him as "my Shepherd." Thus the Bible is filled with concrete images from Hebrew culture: God is our Father and we are his children, God is the Potter and we are the clay, Jesus is the Lamb killed on Passover, heaven is an oasis in the desert, and hell is the city sewage dump.

Many of the Bible's images occur first during the exodus: Israel as God's bride, God as shepherd, the desert as a metaphor for life's difficult experiences, God as living water, God as king, God carrying his people on eagle's wings, the saving blood of the lamb. The Hebrews experienced these and many more familiar images as they left Egypt, spent forty years in the desert, and then entered the Promised Land.

The text frequently describes the people themselves, the descendants of Abraham, as "Hebrews," which probably originated from the Egyptian *habiru* meaning "dusty ones" (a reference to their desert origins). Genesis refers to Abraham as "the Hebrew" (Genesis 14:13), and after God gave Jacob the name *Israel*, the text also calls his descendants *Israelites*. The term *Jew* is not used until much later in history (see the books of Nehemiah and Esther). We will generally use the word *Hebrew* because that is how the people were known in the land of Egypt.

The Hebrew text refers to the land God promised to Abraham as *Canaan* or *Israel*. The Christian text calls it *Judea*. After the Second Jewish Revolt (AD 132 – 135), it was known as *Palestine*. Each of these names resulted from historical events that took place in the land at the time the terms were coined.

One of the earliest designations of the Promised Land, *Canaan*, probably meant "purple," referring to the dye produced from the shells of murex shellfish along the coast of Phoenicia. In the ancient world, this famous dye was used to color garments worn by royalty, and the word for the color referred to the people who produced the dye and purple cloth. Hence, in the Bible, *Canaanite* refers to a "trader" or "merchant" (Zechariah 14:21), as well as to a person from the "land of purple," or Canaan.

Israel, another designation for the Promised Land, derives from the patriarch Jacob. His descendants were known as the Hebrews as well as the children of Israel. After they conquered Canaan during the time of Joshua, the name of the people, *Israel,* became the designation for the land itself (in the same way it had with the Canaanites). When the nation split following the death of Solomon, the name Israel was applied to the northern kingdom and its territory, while the southern land was called Judah. After the fall of the northern kingdom to the Assyrians in 722 BC, the entire land was again called Israel.

During the time of Jesus, the land that had been the nation of Judah was called *Judea* (which means "Jewish"). Because of the influence the people of Judea had over the rest of the land, the land itself was called Judea. The Romans divided the land into several provinces: Judea, Samaria, and Galilee (the three main divisions during Jesus' time); Gaulanitis, the Decapolis, and Perea (east of the Jordan River);

and Idumaea (Edom) and Nabatea (in the south). Later during the Roman era (about one hundred years after Jesus' death), the land was called *Palestine*. Although the Egyptians had referred to the land where the Philistines lived as *Palestine* long before Roman times, the Roman emperor Hadrian popularized the term as part of his campaign to eliminate Jewish influence in the area.

Today the names *Israel* and *Palestine* are often used to designate the land God gave to Abraham. Both terms are politically charged. *Palestine* is used by Arabs living in the central part of the country, and *Israel* is used by Jews to indicate the political State of Israel. In this study, *Israel* is used in the biblical sense. This does not indicate a political statement regarding the current struggle in the Middle East, but best reflects the biblical designation for the land.

Present-day Egypt is a beautiful and advanced country, and we do not identify the "Egyptians" of the Bible as identical to the Egyptians of today any more than we would think of the present prime minister of Egypt as the descendant of the Pharaohs. Nor do we draw any political conclusions regarding relationships between the modern state of Israel and the country of Egypt. Throughout the production of this study, we were warmly welcomed and treated with great hospitality in both countries. Our goal is to study God's work with his Hebrew people as he freed them from slavery in ancient Egypt.

Establishing the Historic and Geographic Setting

When studying the exodus of the Hebrews from Egypt, it is natural to ask, "When did that event occur?" Or, to ask it another way, "Who was the Pharaoh 'who did not know about Joseph'?" (Exodus 1:8). There are two basic theories.[2] One places the biblical event in the eighteenth Egyptian dynasty around 1450 BC, during the reign of Pharaohs such as Thutmose (3) or Amenhotep (2).[3] The other places it in the nineteenth dynasty, during the reign of Ramses the Great (1213 – 1279 BC).[4] Significant textual and scientific support exists for each perspective.

Although I have my opinion on the matter, this study does not attempt in any way to argue for one position or the other. The foundational position for this study is that the exodus occurred as the Bible describes it. Since the Bible does not name the Pharaoh (a word similar to *king* in English), God apparently did not believe this fact to be central to his message. However, in much the same way that one studies ancient languages or uses a good commentary, it is helpful to study specific cultural settings in order to better understand the biblical text. Thus this study focuses on Pharaoh Ramses the Great, not because he was the Pharaoh of the exodus but because he is the epitome of all Pharaohs. Whoever the Pharaoh of the exodus was, we can be sure he wanted and tried to become like Ramses the Great. By focusing our efforts in this way, we will gain a sense of the culture of the time of the exodus (the two theories are relatively close in time anyway) without the burden of the controversy regarding specific dates.

I hold a similar position regarding the route of the exodus. There are many proposed routes and this study does not seek to support one over another. Rather, I have chosen for this study the type of terrain and culture that would represent whichever route the Hebrews took. If knowing the support for the varying points of view is important to you, other studies should be consulted.

God Reclaims His World through History

From the beginning, God planned to reclaim his world from the chaos of sin. He revealed his plan to restore shalom to his creation to Noah, Abraham, Isaac, Jacob, and their families. The books of the Torah, which tell the creation and exodus stories, revealed to the Hebrews who God is, who they were, and who they needed to become. Thus the Torah is God's blueprint describing the role he desires his people to play in his plan of restoration. It forms the foundation of all future acts of God recorded throughout the Bible.

The Hebrews were to be witnesses of God's plan to reclaim his world. Their interaction with the Egyptians and their king, Pharaoh, certainly revealed the nature of the creator of the universe and his desire for his creation (Exodus 8:10; 9:13 – 14). After they reclaimed the Promised Land, the descendants of the Hebrews made God known to many nations as people from all over the world traveled through Israel.

Although his people often have failed in their mission to live righteously and reveal the one true God — *Yahweh*, God continues to use humans as instruments of his redemption. The mission of God's people today is the same one he gave to the ancient Hebrews and Israelites: to live obediently *within* the world so that through us *the world may know that our God is the one true God.* Living by faith is not a vague, otherworldly experience; rather, it is being faithful to God in whatever place and time he has put us.

The message of the Scriptures is eternal and unchanging, and the mission of God's people remains the same, but the circumstances of the people of the Bible are unique to their times. Consequently, we most clearly understand God's truth when we know the cultural context within which he spoke and acted and the perception of the people with whom he communicated. This does not mean that God's revelation is misunderstood if we don't know the cultural context. Rather, by cultivating our understanding of the world in which God's story was told, we will begin to see it as an actual place with real people and a real culture. When we view God's story in this way, we often discover truth we would not see otherwise.

As we explore the Egypt of the Bible and study the people and events in their geographic and historic contexts, we will discover the *who*, *what*, and *where* of the exodus story and will better understand the *why*. By learning how to think and approach life as Amram, Jochebed, Moses, Aaron, Miriam, Joshua, Phineas, and other Hebrews, we will discover that we too experience "Egypt" in our lives. And, like the ancient Hebrews, we will discover that it is much easier for God to get us out of Egypt than to get Egypt out of us.

The intent of this study is to enter the world of the Hebrews and familiarize ourselves with their culture and the cultures of their day so that we may fully apply the Bible's message to our lives. We will seek to better understand God's revealed mission for the events and characters of the exodus from Egypt and the forty years of training (testing) in the desert so that we, in turn, will better understand God's purpose in Jesus' life and in our lives. Our purpose is to follow God's intent as revealed to Ezekiel:

Son of man, look with your eyes and hear with your ears and pay attention to everything I am going to show you, for that is why you have been brought here. Tell the house of Israel everything you see.

Ezekiel 40:4

"Let my people go!"

These words still ring with power and clarity after more than 3,000 years. God still seeks to free his people and his world from the chaos that sin has brought to it. Now he invites you, as he invited Israel, the Egyptians, and even Pharaoh, to experience the freedom to serve and worship (in Hebrew, both words are the same!) him as the one, true God.

THE LORD WHO HEALS YOU: MARAH AND ELIM

Exodus 15:22–27

The Hebrews' exodus from Egypt is the story of God fulfilling the promises of his covenant with Abraham (see Genesis 15). But that story had a bigger purpose than merely to release Abraham's enslaved descendants from the oppression of their Egyptian masters. Rather, God intended Abraham's offspring to become his witnesses, his model people. God desired them to live in such an exemplary manner that all other peoples would come to know his name and find salvation in him, and in the Messiah who was yet to come.

In spite of God's spectacular acts of power demonstrated through the plagues, the Hebrews' redemption from Egypt was only the first step in a long journey of training. To become God's witnesses, the Hebrews (Israel) needed to learn to trust him in all circumstances and to live by faith in his word. They needed God's laws to guide them and a sacrificial system through which they could receive forgiveness for their wrongdoing and their failures. They needed to learn to worship God by living according to his commands so that every aspect of their lives reflected his righteousness and demonstrated his deep, compassionate love for the poor, the suffering, and the broken. In short, the Hebrews needed a complete and thorough reeducation to purge the ways of Egypt from their hearts and lives and to replace them with the righteous, compassionate character of those who walk with God.

So God led them from the comfort and abundance of the fertile Nile Valley into the harsh, barren environment of the desert. There his people were challenged to affirm their newly rekindled faith and to practice living it out. Whenever they failed (and they often did), God forgave them and put before them another "test" — another opportunity to choose to walk with him.

Although many people today view the Israelites' desert experiences through the lens of their failures, there is so much more to their forty-year wilderness story! Despite their obvious failures, God loved and provided for them. They experienced God's presence and protection through daily miracles — manna and quail, water from the rock, pillars of fire and cloud. In fact, the prophet Jeremiah declared in tender language that God fondly remembered the wilderness years as his courtship with his beloved bride (Jeremiah 2:1 – 2). By God's grace, the Israelite children reared in the desert were better prepared than their parents to live in a manner that revealed their God to the world. They were better prepared to walk with God and step into their place in his plan to reclaim the world from the chaos of sin.

Almost every foundational element of faith known in the Bible is rooted in Israel's awe-filled experiences in the desert wilderness. These experiences were so central to the identity of God's people during Jesus' day, that Jesus — God's "second" firstborn son (Israel, according to Exodus 4:22, was God's "first" firstborn son) — also went to the desert ... for *forty* days! The thrilling stories of those experiences also remind us that the legacy of the ancient Israelites now rests on our shoulders. God desires that all who follow him — Jew or Gentile — not only *tell* but *show* the nations his nature by the way we live.

Thus the ancient Israelites contributed to preparing us for our walk with God! And, just as he did with them, God still leads us into the "desert" where he shapes us — the body of Christ — into the people he wants us to be. We should not be surprised when life is difficult and harsh, filled with struggles and testing. God provides us with opportunities to trust him fully, obey him wholeheartedly, and practice being who he has called us to be. We join the ancient people of God in the desert because in their sandal prints we discover a map for our walk with God. Their failures are our lessons; their victories are our inspiration. Through their struggles, we stand on a firm foundation to fulfill our mission as God's witnesses to a broken, sinful world.

Opening Thoughts (3 minutes)

The Very Words of God

> Remember how the LORD your God led you all the way in the desert these forty years, to humble you and to test you in order to know what was in your heart, whether or not you would keep his commands.

Deuteronomy 8:2

Think About It

The difficulties of testing are nothing new to us. Teachers test their students to discover how thoroughly they understand their lessons; commanders test their troops to assess their strength, agility, and preparedness for battle; parents test their children's obedience and decision making to evaluate their maturity.

What are some of the specific ways by which we "test" a person's preparedness to fulfill his or her future responsibilities, and how might the person who is being tested perceive those experiences?

DVD Notes (32 minutes)

Into the desert—why?

To humble

To test

One bitter well—the first big test

A lesson about "sticks"

The rest of the story—twelve wells, seventy palms

DVD Discussion (6 minutes)

1. What kinds of experiences do you think were a part of daily life in the fertile Nile Delta, and what kinds of experiences do you think were a part of daily life in the extremes of the vast, barren Sinai desert?

In what ways might a person's lifestyle choices and emotional and spiritual responses to life differ in each of these environments?

What insight does this give you into why God wanted the Hebrews to leave the Nile Delta and spend some time living in the desert?

THE CONTRASTS BETWEEN THE LUSH NILE DELTA AND THE BARREN SINAI DESERT ARE EXTREME. PERHAPS IT SHOULDN'T SURPRISE US THAT THE ISRAELITES EXPRESSED FEAR ABOUT WHAT THEY WOULD EAT AND DRINK — AND EVEN THOUGHT THEY WOULD DIE IN THE DESERT.

2. Most of us have never seen a desert, much less felt the relentless, baking heat of its vast, barren expanse, so it is hard to imagine what it would be like to travel on foot through the Sinai Desert. When we live much of our lives in climate-controlled buildings where a drink of pure water — either hot or cold — is just a few steps away, it's difficult to imagine what it would be like to be hot, thirsty, and days away from a water source.

Look at the map, "The Land of the Exodus," and consider where the Israelites might have been after two to three days' walk from the crossing of the sea. We know that they did not take the Way to the Land of the Philistines (along the Mediterranean), so trace the other possible routes across the Sinai or along the Red Sea toward the tip of the peninsula. Considering that all of the land they had walked through had been desert wilderness — hills, rock, gravel, sand, mountains, a

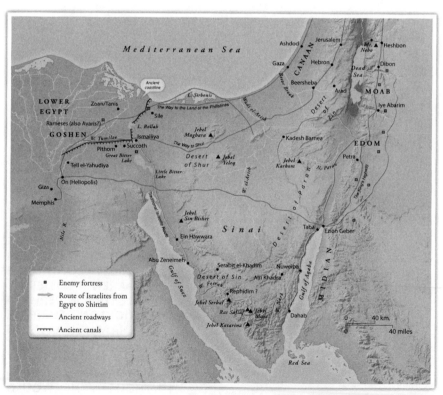

THE LAND OF THE EXODUS

few scattered shrubs in the wadis — how much do you think they longed for fresh water?

3. For a moment, try to put yourself in the sandals of one of the Israelites at Marah. They were two to three days from their last source of water, in a place they had never been before, and God had led them to water that they couldn't even drink! What did God's "test" at Marah's bitter well reveal about what was foremost in their hearts? What might God's "test" have revealed about what is foremost in your heart?

4. In light of the fact that God previously had used Moses' staff as an instrument of his mighty power, what is significant about God choosing to use a different piece of wood to make the water sweet? What impact might this experience have had on Moses and why?

FOR GREATER UNDERSTANDING
The Geography of the Exodus

One of the most debated geographic issues of the Hebrew Bible is the location of Mount Sinai and the route from Goshen the Hebrews took to get there. The Torah clearly and precisely describes the exodus from Egypt, and this study accepts the story provided in the Torah as completely accurate. Although the Torah names several cities and places on that journey, it does not provide sufficient data to correlate with current archaeological information and establish definitive locations. Thus many historical and geographical

continued on next page . . .

questions concerning the exact route of the exodus remain unanswered and open to debate.

Fortunately, this study does not depend on our knowing all of the specific locations and routes. Our emphasis is best expressed by the Middle Eastern saying, "It is not where an event occurred that is important but where it is remembered." Whereas knowing a specific setting for a biblical story often enhances and enriches our understanding, the text itself provides the lesson. So our purpose is to explore the events and God's revelation through them, *not to make a case for a particular geographical theory*. Therefore, the locations filmed for this study generally represent the places where the story occurred and are similar to the Torah's descriptions but no attempt has been made to "prove" that these are the actual places.

That being said, nearly all scholars agree that the Hebrews did not take "The Way to the Land of the Philistines." That route, along the Mediterranean coast on the northwestern edge of the Sinai Peninsula, was part of the ancient

COMPARED TO THE HEBREWS, THE PHILISTINES WERE REMARKABLY SOPHISTICATED. COMPARED TO THE EGYPTIANS, HOWEVER, THEY WERE RELATIVELY WEAK. SO WHY WOULD GOD LEAD HIS PEOPLE INTO THE DESERT RATHER THAN BY THE WAY OF THE PHILISTINES IN ORDER TO AVOID A BATTLE? GOD HAD JUST DESTROYED THE POWER OF EGYPT, AND HE COULD HAVE DESTROYED THE PHILISTINES AS WELL, BUT HE APPARENTLY EXPECTED GREATER PARTICIPATION FROM HIS PEOPLE IN THIS NEXT BATTLE, AND THEY WERE NOT YET READY.

trade route and military road that passed through Canaan (later, Israel) and connected Egypt to the region of Babylon and the Tigris and Euphrates rivers. God did not lead the Hebrews that way because they were not ready to face the strong military presence of the Philistines who inhabited the region at that time (Exodus 13:17).

Significant Jewish and Christian scholars have presented evidence for three major theories regarding the location of Mount Sinai and the exodus route: northwest Saudi Arabia or southern Jordan; northern Sinai Peninsula; and the traditional location in the mountains of southern Sinai. At least twenty Mount Sinai locations have been argued by scholars, and well-meaning amateurs have presented theories that contribute little to understanding the text.

Video for this study was filmed in the vicinity of the traditional route along the Gulf of Suez to Wadi Feiran and the Granite Highlands and portrays Jebel Katarina and Jebel Musa as Mount Sinai. These locations represent typical desert features—wells, roads, mountains—that research reveals are similar to those mentioned in the Torah. Bible students who are interested in evaluating evidence for a particular location or route should refer to sources that have this as their intent.[1]

Small Group Bible Discovery and Discussion (13 minutes)

The Lord Led You

God promised Moses that he would bring the Hebrews out of Egypt and into a land "flowing with milk and honey," the same land he had promised to Abraham, Isaac, and Jacob (Exodus 3:8; 6:8). By the most direct route, this land was less than two hundred miles from Egypt—a journey that would have taken less than three weeks. But God knew his people were discouraged and their faith was weak, so he had another route in mind. Via this route, it took forty days just to reach Mount Sinai! By choosing a longer, more difficult route, God provided opportunities for the Hebrews to learn how to be obedient, active participants with him in his bigger plan to reclaim his world.

1. To the Hebrews, who for generations had lived in the abundant and well-watered Nile Delta, the desert was an unknown, frightening place of chaos and danger. What compelled them to go into this strange, hostile place, and how did they know which way to go? (See Exodus 13:21 – 22; 15:22.)

NOTE: The Hebrew word that is translated "led" in the NIV (Exodus 15:22) is *nasa,* which carries the meaning of "caus-

THE VAST SINAI DESERT BEGINS WHERE THE WAVES OF THE RED SEA LAP THE SHORE. HOW MIGHT YOU HAVE RESPONDED TO THE NEWS THAT *THIS* WAS THE WAY TO THE PROMISED LAND?

ing, driving, or forcing." So the text at least hints that the Israelites may have in some way hesitated or resisted stepping forward into the desert.

2. What was the desert like, and how did the Israelites feel about being there? (See Numbers 20:1 – 5; Deuteronomy 1:19; 8:15; Jeremiah 2:6.)

    How is their response like or unlike your response when it seems that God has placed you in difficult, challenging circumstances?

3. God clearly expressed his intent and purpose for leading his people into the desert. (See Exodus 19:3 – 6; Deuteronomy 8:2 – 5, 16.)

    a. What did God want to accomplish in the hearts and lives of his people, and how would the desert experience contribute to this training?

    b. What images did God use to describe his relationship with his people and, therefore, his motivation for leading them into the desert?

    c. What do these images say to you about how highly God values his relationship with his people?

Faith Lesson (5 minutes)

The desert is the place where people are forced to live one moment at a time. When we, or people we love, experience difficult, "desert" times, we often struggle to understand why God would lead us into painful circumstances. We may question why God would want us to be in the desert. We may feel confused when we are thrust into circumstances that appear — at least to us — to contradict God's loving nature. This was true of the Israelites, it was true of the early Christian believers, and it is true of us. Yet God, who dearly loves all who follow him and truly desires that "in the end it might go well" for us, also leads us along difficult paths in dangerous territory that humble us and test us in order to know what is in our hearts.

1. Consider the experience of the apostle Paul, who was tormented by what he called a "thorn in my flesh" that he begged God to take away from him (2 Corinthians 12:7 – 10).

   a. What did the testing from this desert reveal about the apostle Paul's heart — to him as well as to God — and what did it allow him to experience?

   b. To what extent would you want to experience this level of intimacy, trust, and commitment in your relationship with God?

2. What has been your personal experience with God on a roundabout "journey" or in a vast and dreadful "desert"?

   How much did you complain and long for the good things you had back in "Egypt"?

What did you discover about what was really in your heart? Fear? Lack of faith? Rebellion? Selfishness?

In which way(s) did the desires of your heart change as a result of that experience?

What of great value would you have missed out on if you had taken a "shortcut" or avoided the desert altogether?

3. If you are on a difficult path or in the midst of an intense time in the desert right now, what strength and encouragement do you gain from the experiences of the Israelites and others who have gone into the desert before you?

Closing (1 minute)

Read Deuteronomy 8:2 – 5 aloud together: "Remember how the LORD your God led you all the way in the desert these forty years, to humble you and to test you in order to know what was in your heart, whether or not you would keep his commands. He humbled you, causing you to hunger and then feeding you with manna, which neither you nor your fathers had known, to teach you that man does not live on bread alone but on every word that comes from the mouth of the LORD. Your clothes did not wear out and your feet did not swell during these forty years. Know then in your heart that as a man disciplines his son, so the LORD your God disciplines you."

Then pray about the "tests" that you and other people are facing. Ask God to give you the strength to obey him fully and the faith to live on every word that comes from him. Thank him for his unfailing love for you, a love that includes training you to follow him with all your heart, all your soul, and all your strength.

Memorize

Remember how the Lord your God led you all the way in the desert these forty years, to humble you and to test you in order to know what was in your heart, whether or not you would keep his commands. He humbled you, causing you to hunger and then feeding you with manna, which neither you nor your fathers had known, to teach you that man does not live on bread alone but on every word that comes from the mouth of the Lord. Your clothes did not wear out and your feet did not swell during these forty years. Know then in your heart that as a man disciplines his son, so the Lord your God disciplines you.

Deuteronomy 8:2 – 5

Tested and Trained to Be God's Message

In-Depth Personal Study Sessions

Day One | Humbled and Tested to Fulfill God's Purpose

The Very Words of God

> *Be careful to follow every command I am giving you today, so that you may live and increase and may enter and possess the land that the Lord promised on oath to your forefathers. Remember how the Lord your God led you all the way in the desert these forty years, to humble you and to test you in order to know what was in your heart, whether or not you would keep his commands.*

> *Deuteronomy 8:1 – 2*

Bible Discovery

Tested to Reveal What Was in Their Hearts

From the time he created the first humans, male and female, God desired to partner with his people in caring for the earth and "increasing" their numbers and influence (Genesis 1:28). In the garden of Eden, the crafty serpent quickly exposed the weakness in the hearts of God's partners. They disobeyed the command of God and strayed from his purpose (Genesis 2:15 – 17; 3:1 – 7). But God never gave up on his redemptive plan. Once he freed the Hebrews from slavery under Pharaoh, it was a new beginning — a new chapter in God's plan to restore shalom to his creation. But what was in their hearts? Were they fully devoted to obeying God's commands and fulfilling his purpose, or would they insist on going their own way?

1. What might prevent the Israelites from "increasing" and fulfilling their role as God's partners in the land he had promised to their forefathers? (See Deuteronomy 8:1.)

2. What process did God use to know whether or not the Israelites would keep his commands? (See Deuteronomy 8:2.)

3. People who value independence, material success, or personal accomplishment may have some difficulty understanding why God would find it necessary to "humble" his people. Consider the meaning of the word in the following contexts:

   a. *Deuteronomy 8:2:* God apparently wanted to humble his people to know whether or not they would obey him. In what ways do you think the response of humble people to God's commands might differ from that of people who trust in their own strength and capabilities?

   b. *Exodus 1:11:* The same Hebrew word for "humble" is translated as "oppress" in the NIV, and it describes how the Egyptians treated the Hebrew slaves. How did the Egyptians' intent in humbling the Hebrews differ from God's intent?

   c. *Leviticus 23:26 – 29:* The Hebrew word for "humble" is translated "deny himself" in verse 29, which means to "humble" or "lower oneself." What is the intent of humbling in this example?

DID YOU KNOW?

In Deuteronomy 8:2:

- *Humble* means to "bring down" or "lower" someone.
- *Test* implies proving the quality of someone by experience, not just by intellectual assent. Note that this testing is *not* the same as enticing someone to do wrong.
- *Know* (*yada*) means to know something, but to know it experientially, not just intellectually. Knowing in this way implies the experience of a relationship having deep emotional interaction, fervent loyalty, and unfailing commitment. It is used to describe the intimacy of the marriage relationship. When applied to knowing God, it means a close personal relationship resulting in an experiential understanding of and connection to God's nature and purpose.

4. Jewish sages struggled with the idea that God "tested" the hearts of his people because they believed the text indicates that God already knew what was in the hearts of his people. What insight into God's testing of his people to know what was in their hearts do you gain from Isaiah 40:27 – 29; 42:6 – 9?

As a result of God's testing, who else besides God would "know" what was in the hearts of the Israelites?

What do you think might have been the value in God giving the Israelites the opportunity to prove the quality of their faith through difficult experiences?

FOR GREATER UNDERSTANDING
A Personal Story from Ray Vander Laan

By God's grace, a routine physical revealed that I had previously experienced a silent heart attack. The condition of my heart required triple bypass surgery. As I was wheeled into the operating room, I knew there was a possibility, however low, that I might not survive. Yet I vividly realized that I was not afraid of death. I had the clear sense that God was present and providing his grace to face the future. I always had believed that God would provide strength during such a time, but prior to that day I had never *experienced* his strength in that way. Knowing what was in my heart on that day still gives me great confidence and comfort because I experienced God's grace so intensely. That experience is a reminder to me of the value of knowing what is in my heart and the value of being tested in order to discover it.

5. God's testing of the Israelites in the desert showed that they were not wholeheartedly devoted to him, but what happened as he continued to humble and train them in the desert? (See Jeremiah 2:2 – 3.)

POINT TO PONDER
"Man Shall Not Live by Bread Alone"

God wanted his people to learn that "man does not live on bread alone but on every word that comes from the mouth of the LORD." Some Jewish scholars believe that God intended Israel to live by God's word in everything—including what is appropriate to eat, and when. In Egypt, by God's blessing, the Hebrews enjoyed a variety of foods in abundance. They probably thought they would be able to choose what to eat, and when, in the desert as well. But God was teaching them that all of life was to be a response of obedience to him and to his words of leading—including their food. If God was leading and natural food was not available, he would feed them. They had to live in complete trust and dependence on every word that came from his mouth, and if they did not, God warned that there would be consequences.

God still leads by his word, so what does it mean for us to depend on it—to live by every word that comes from his mouth—today? Should we eat what is not healthy if it violates God's word to care for our bodies? Should we eat more than we need if other people do not have enough? Are there areas of our lives (jobs, scholarships, talents, etc.) for which we take credit and overlook God's provision? In what sense does every choice provide an opportunity for us to respond to the leading of God's word?

When Satan tempted him in the desert, Jesus quoted Deuteronomy 8:3: "Man does not live on bread alone, but on every word that comes from the mouth of God." Jesus literally chose to live by every word that came from God's mouth (Matthew 4:1 – 4), including God's choice of when and what to eat. How can we follow his example and learn to live by every word that comes from God's mouth?

Reflection

Like the Israelites, God's people today face times of humbling and testing in the "desert." We are not likely to face the exact circumstances they did, but we will certainly encounter our weaknesses, our inadequacy to solve the problems we face, our vulnerability apart from God's saving grace, our uncertainty about outcomes, and our fears about the entire experience. Romans 5:3 – 5 and James 1:2 – 4, 12 describe the purpose of these trials and testing.

> In what ways is the testing described in these passages similar to what the Israelites experienced in the desert? What is its purpose, its value, its impact?

Think of the times when God has humbled and tested you. What did you learn from these experiences about what was really in your heart, and in what ways did what you discovered surprise you, disappoint you, challenge you?

What did you discover about your trust in God and your devotion to him?

What did you discover about God's love and commitment to you?

Which aspects of your daily life with God became stronger as a result of that time of testing?

If you viewed life's difficult circumstances as one way by which God trains and prepares you to be a partner in his plan of redemption, how would it help you not only *face* such times but *benefit* from them?

To what extent will you take the Israelites' story to heart and consider how, with God's help, times of testing in your life can be a springboard to:

Knowing and trusting God experientially?

Discovering what you really believe?

Strengthing your faith and your commitment to walk with God?

Memorize

Consider it pure joy, my brothers, whenever you face trials of many kinds, because you know that the testing of your faith develops perseverance. Perseverance must finish its work so that you may be mature and complete, not lacking anything.

James 1:2 – 4

Day Two | Thirst in the Desert

The Very Words of God

Then Moses led Israel from the Red Sea and they went into the Desert of Shur. For three days they traveled in the desert without finding water.

Exodus 15:22

Bible Discovery

In the Heat of the Desert, Israel Forgets

So much had changed for the former Hebrew slaves in a short period of time. God had delivered them from the hand of Pharaoh and had demonstrated his awesome power at the Red Sea. In response, the Israelites had stood on the shore and with wholehearted enthusiasm affirmed God's reign over their lives. As a community, they danced for joy before their majestic God. But once they journeyed into the dry, barren desert and found themselves helpless even to find good water to drink, they quickly forgot God's goodness and faithfulness toward them.

1. What incomparable miracle had God accomplished on behalf of his people at the Red Sea? (See Exodus 14:10, 21 – 30.)

   How had they responded to him? (See Exodus 14:31; 15:20 – 21.)

   What did they expect their God to do for them in the future? (See Exodus 15:13 – 18.)

2. How far had the Hebrews expected to travel into the desert, and how soon after crossing the Red Sea did they reach the well at Marah? (See Exodus 3:18; 5:3; 8:27; 15:22 – 23.)

   What do you think they might have expected to find at Marah?

   To what extent do you think they anticipated a crisis at this point in their journey?

FOR GREATER UNDERSTANDING
A Well in the Desert

No one knows for certain the location of Marah or the well with its bitter water. Suggested locations are similar to this well in the Sinai Peninsula, which is

in the vicinity of the "traditional" exodus route. Such wells tend to be located in small oases where a few palm trees suggest the presence of ground water near the surface.

Imagine the entire nation of Israel gathered around such a well in the hope of finding life-giving water! Picturing this setting in the midst of a hostile desert environment helps us to appreciate the difficulty of finding food and water for thousands of people.

3. Exodus 15:23 – 24 describes how the Israelites responded to their first crisis after leaving the Red Sea.

   a. How do you think they could have forgotten all of God's amazing miracles on their behalf *just three days* after leaving the Red Sea?

   b. How had the barren desert already affected them and their sense of confidence in Moses' leadership and God's provision?

   c. What did their response to the bitter water at Marah reveal about what was foremost in their hearts? To what extent was this part of God's plan?

   d. If you had been there, how easily would you have become disheartened by this turn of events and forgotten all that God had done for you?

4. Deuteronomy 11:8 – 15 explains ways in which life in the Promised Land would differ from life in Egypt, and Joshua 24:14 adds to the emphasis that the way of life in Egypt had significant spiritual consequences for God's people.

   a. How might the fact that the Hebrews watered their own fields in Egypt have affected their awareness of and dependence on God for their survival?

b. To what had they appeared to attribute their survival in Egypt, and what impact did this have on their commitment to and confidence in the God of their ancestors?

c. On what would their survival and well-being in the Promised Land depend, and what was the key to their receiving what they needed?

Reflection

We can easily see the flaws in the hearts of the Israelites when, at risk of dying from thirst in the sun-baked desert, they seem to have completely forgotten all that God had just done for them. But perhaps we are more like them than we realize.

In Egypt, they had become comfortable in planting and watering their fields and reaping abundant harvests. Perhaps they had come to believe that they were responsible for their survival and that God had little to do with the details of their daily lives. If that was the case, their response to the situation in Marah is not so surprising.

How do you think you would have responded in that situation if:

deep in your heart you believed that solving the problem was up to you?

you were not absolutely certain that you could entrust yourself (and your family's survival) to God's loving provision?

Think of a circumstance in your life that you felt you could not handle (a natural disaster, a devastating illness, an overwhelming financial need, or some other crisis).

How did you respond to the situation, to other people involved, and to God?

Was your initial reaction to trust God with your whole heart or to panic, and why did you respond that way?

How quickly did your heart become so overwhelmed that you forgot the care and blessing God had provided for you in the past?

In which "desert" area(s) of life do you find it particularly hard to trust God?

In what ways does God's testing of the Israelites at Marah help you to better understand and respond differently when faced with these types of difficulties?

How might focusing your attention on what God has done — and is doing — strengthen your heart to trust in him during difficult times?

Day Three | Israel Discovers the Meaning of Marah

The Very Words of God

> *Moses led Israel from the Red Sea and they went into the Desert of*
> *Shur.... When they came to Marah, they could not drink its water*
> *because it was bitter. (That is why the place is called Marah.) So the*
> *people grumbled against Moses, saying, "What are we to drink?"*
>
> *Exodus 15:22 – 24*

Bible Discovery

Bitter Water, Defiant Disobedience

Biblical names are often laden with meaning, and *Marah* is no
exception. God guided the thirsty Hebrews to the well at Marah.
Perhaps they saw a few scattered palm trees in the distance and
quickened their pace in excitement. Finally they would have
life-giving water! But what a disappointment: the water at Marah
was too bitter to drink! What were they going to do? What would
happen to them?

1. When the Israelites learned that the water of Marah was bitter and unfit to drink, what attitude did they exhibit toward
   Moses and God? (See Exodus 15:23 – 24.)

   God, through Moses, clearly had led his people to Marah.
   What do you think was his reason for leading them to bitter
   water — water that was unfit for its intended purpose?

In what way(s) might the bitter water have illustrated the attitude of the Israelites' hearts and their ability to be partners in God's plan of redemption?

2. In Hebrew, *marah* not only means "bitter" but when applied to people it implies an attitude of "complete opposition" or "deliberately obstinate and defiant disobedience." What insight into what God wanted to accomplish in the hearts of the Israelites do you gain from the following examples of those whom the text calls *marah*?

    a. Genesis 26:34–35 ("source of grief" comes from *marah*)

    b. Numbers 20:24 ("rebelled" comes from *marah*)

    c. Deuteronomy 9:7 ("rebellious" comes from *marah*)

    d. Deuteronomy 21:18–21 (*marah* is translated "rebellious")

3. After the people grumbled against Moses, what did God do to meet their need? (See Exodus 15:25–26.)

What do you think God wanted the Israelites to learn — not just intellectually but also experientially — from this "bitter" experience that became "sweet"?

For what reason do you think God provided commands for the Hebrews immediately after their complaints and the miracle of the sweetened water?

What might be the connection between this "bitter" experience and the openness of the Israelites' hearts and minds to obeying God's commands?

What does this miracle say to you about how tenderly God loves his people and the kind of relationship he longs to have with them?

Reflection

Each of us chooses how we will respond to God when we are pushed beyond our limits and see no possible resolution to our crisis. Whether we respond with defiant complaints or trusting confidence is up to us. God, who knows our hearts, longs for us to trust him when things seem to be falling apart as well as when he provides "sweet" refreshment.

When has God led you to a place like Marah, and what did you experience there?

How did you respond to the difficulty, disappointment, and/
or danger of that place — with an attitude of trust and confidence in God or an attitude of *marah*?

What do you think God wanted to show you and teach you
through that experience?

How responsive a student were you, and where did God lead
you next as a result of what you learned?

How does the fact that God used a time of suffering to break
Egypt's hold on the Hebrews — whose hearts trusted in their
own provision and doubted his — influence your understanding
of what God desires for you?

The text ends the story of Marah with God's plea for obedience
and his promise: "I am the LORD, who heals you" (Exodus 15:26).
How might the entire wilderness experience of the Israelites be
God's way of healing the hearts of his people so that they would
no longer respond out of the brokenness of *marah* but with
wholehearted trust and obedience before him?

How might this perspective influence your response the
next time you are tempted to respond to God with *marah*?

Memorize

> *Who is wise? He will realize these things.*
> *Who is discerning? He will understand them.*
> *The ways of the* L<small>ORD</small> *are right;*
> *the righteous walk in them,*
> *but the rebellious stumble in them.*

> *Hosea 14:9*

Day Four | The Power of That Stick!

The Very Words of God

> *Moses cried out to the* L<small>ORD</small>, *and the* L<small>ORD</small> *showed him a piece of wood.*
> *He threw it into the water, and the water became sweet.*

> *Exodus 15:25*

Bible Discovery

God Uses the Ordinary to Accomplish His Mighty Purpose

The Bible records many examples of God's spectacular, miraculous acts: the Creation, Isaac's birth, the plagues in Egypt, the parting of the Red Sea, dramatic healings, the routing of pagan armies, the opening of prison doors, etc. The situation God's people faced at Marah certainly required God's miraculous intervention, but as he often does, God chose to use surprisingly ordinary means to accomplish his purpose. Even Moses may have been surprised by what God did and learned something new as a result of this training session in the desert.

1. What symbol did God instruct Moses (and Aaron) to use to display God's miraculous power before Pharaoh, and why do you think God chose it? (See Exodus 4:1 – 5, 14 – 17, 20; 7:14 – 18; 9:22 – 23; 10:12 – 13; 14:15 – 16, 21, 26.)

In light of all of these experiences, how much confidence might Moses have placed in himself and this symbol when he arrived at Marah?

Given his role in leading the Israelites through the desert, how important do you think it was for Moses to recognize his total dependence on God and to wholeheartedly obey every command God gave?

DID YOU KNOW?

The Hebrew word *ze'akah*, translated "cried out" in Exodus 15:25, implies a loud, desperate wail caused by great pain. Throughout the Bible, God responds with power when he hears such a cry. He responded to that cry from the Hebrew slaves (Exodus 2:23–25) before they even recognized him as their God, and from the escaping Hebrews when Pharaoh's army trapped them against the Red Sea (Exodus 14:10). He responded to the cry from Moses at Marah, and he still responds to such cries today.

2. After Moses cried out to God, what did God tell him to pick up? (See Exodus 15:25.)

Why might Moses have been surprised to learn that he was not to use the staff that God had used previously in doing miracles?

Do you think Moses might have wondered what God could be saying to him through this unusual command? Why or why not?

DID YOU KNOW?

During his forty years as a shepherd, Moses had become an expert in desert survival. But at Marah, he—like the Hebrews—evidently needed more training in depending on God alone. That, Jewish thought suggests, is why God chose to use something other than Moses' shepherd staff—the "staff of God"—to sweeten the water.

What did God provide for this amazing miracle? An ordinary piece of wood! The Hebrew word translated "piece of wood" in Exodus 15:25 can be translated "tree," "stalk," "bark," "log," "branch," "piece of wood," "stick," and in four cases the context demands it be translated "staff." Although Moses still had his staff, which had come to represent God's power at work on behalf of his people, God chose an ordinary piece of wood—perhaps a branch, perhaps a chunk of bark—to represent his miraculous power in sweetening the water at Marah.

---

3. It is interesting to note that Jesus also used ordinary things to accomplish the miracle of giving sight to a blind man. (See John 9:1 – 7.)

   a. Would the mud and water from Siloam normally have caused a miracle?

   b. Why, then, do you think Jesus used them in restoring the blind man's sight?

4. God not only uses ordinary things that in and of themselves
    have no ability or power to accomplish the miraculous, he
    also uses "ordinary" people to accomplish his purposes.
    As you read the following passages, note what God accom-
    plished and why it was "out of the ordinary" for that person
    to be a participant in an extraordinary work of God.

Text	Person(s)	What God Accomplished and Why It Was Extraordinary
Gen. 41, 45	Joseph, a slave	
Ex. 3, 12	Moses, a shepherd	
1 Sam. 17	David, a shepherd boy	
Gen. 38, Matt. 1:3	Tamar, a Caananite	
Luke 1:26–38; 2:4–12	Mary, a young woman	
Matt. 4:18–22; 28:16–20	Andrew, John, Peter, James— fishermen	
Luke 8:1–3; Mark 16:1–9	Mary Magdalene, formerly demon-possessed	

Reflection

The story of Marah, where God used an ordinary stick in the hands of an obedient servant to change the water from bitter to sweet (and to initiate a similar change in the hearts of his people), has a powerful message for us today. No matter what our credentials or experience, we too are "ordinary people." But in the hands of God, we can become awesome instruments who are fit to accomplish his mighty purpose.

Centuries after the Israelites moved on from Marah, Paul wrote to God's people in Corinth about who God chooses to accomplish his purposes. (See 1 Corinthians 1:26 – 31.) What is Paul's explanation for why God chooses the weak, the ordinary, and the foolish to accomplish his purposes?

To what extent do you value the "ordinary" people God often chooses as opposed to the wise, the influential, and the noble?

What enables the weak, the ordinary, and the foolish to accomplish God's purposes?

How would you evaluate your tendency to believe in your own power to accomplish great things for God and to forget that he is the source of all power?

How willing are you to be an ordinary "piece of wood" in God's hands?

What changes in your heart attitude and everyday walk with God must you make to become a more fit instrument for him?

Day Five | God Strengthens the Community of His People at Elim

The Very Words of God

> Moses cried out to the LORD, and the LORD showed him a piece of wood. He threw it into the water, and the water became sweet. There the Lord made a decree and a law for them, and there he tested them.... Then they came to Elim, where there were twelve springs and seventy palm trees, and they camped there near the water.
>
> *Exodus 15:25, 27*

Bible Discovery

God Begins Building a Community to Be His Partners

The experience of the Israelites at Marah initiated a new level of participation in their partnership with God. After showing his loving care for them by making the bitter water sweet, God gave them laws and emphasized how important it was for them to listen for his voice and obey his commands. Obedience was God's way to test them and give them opportunities to show that they trusted his word and that their relationship with him was true and faithful. From Marah, God's people moved on to Elim, where there were twelve springs, and from there they set out into the desert.

1. The exact commands God gave to the Israelites after he sweetened the water at Marah are a bit of a mystery. Given the context of when in the Israelites' journey God gave these instructions and what they had just experienced, what do you think these commands might have been about? (See Exodus 15:25 – 26.)

    How important to God were these commands, and how important was the Israelites' obedience to them? How do you know this?

    What did God promise would result if the Israelites obeyed him?

    Why do you think God mentioned the Egyptians in this context, and what do you think he was really communicating to Israel?

2. After God sweetened the water at Marah and gave them "a decree and a law," where did he lead the Israelites, and why would they go there when the water at Marah was drinkable? (See Exodus 15:27.)

THINK ABOUT IT

This well is typical of the few wells in the Sinai desert. It is dug deep into the limestone bedrock where water is found. The upper part is lined with stones to keep dirt out of the well. Just imagine what it would have been like for thousands of desperately thirsty people to obtain water from just *one* well such as this!

The logistics of such an effort suggest that the decree and law God gave to his people at Marah may have involved learning to cooperate together as a community to provide for everyone's needs rather than individuals selfishly meeting their needs at the expense of others. In fact, the Jewish sages have noted that the three crises on the trek to Mount Sinai (Marah, manna, and the second shortage of water) all involved the need to function as a community. Furthermore, the Torah described the Israelites with the plural pronoun on the journey, but used the singular pronoun when they arrived at Mount Sinai. Might it be that God used the journey to Sinai to shape a group of individuals into one community of people?

Although the precise location of Elim is unknown, this wadi near the "traditional" route of the exodus appears similar to the Torah's description of Elim:

"twelve springs [wells] and seventy palm trees." (There are several wells beneath these palm trees, but not exactly twelve springs and seventy palms.)

The Israelites' encampment at Elim provides further hints that the journey to Sinai was, in part, a training ground for God's people to become a community. To the ancient Eastern way of thinking, it is significant that the number twelve (springs) was the number of the community of God's people (Exodus 28:21), and seventy was the number of Jacob's family when they went down to Egypt (Genesis 46:26 – 27). In addition, the word *Elim* means "strength," which adds to the suggestion that God was building and encouraging his community of people.

3. What role did God desire his people to have in the world, and why do you think functioning as a community would be important in fulfilling that role? (See Exodus 19:3 – 6.)

4. Read 1 John 2:3 – 4 and 3:18 – 24, and consider what place obedience to God and true community have among those who claim to know Jesus Christ today.

What does our lack of obedience and love demonstrate?

What impact would a lack of obedience and love have on fulfilling our role in God's plan of redemption?

Reflection

At Marah, God put before the Israelites an extremely difficult challenge that would test their hearts and their willingness to obey his commands and live according to his word. He also began to teach them how they would need to trust and obey him as a community that would fulfill his purposes and experience his blessings.

What in your life has tested your commitment to trust and obey God?

How have you responded, and how did your response impact your life and lives of others?

What did you learn through those experiences about yourself, God, and your relationship with him?

What did you learn through those experiences about the role of the community of God's people in your life to not only encourage you in trust and obedience but in standing as a witness to the world of who God is and what he is doing?

In what ways has your experience of being strengthened by God within a faith community been to you like what the abundant wells and palm trees of Elim were to the Israelites?

What is your commitment to be a part of a community of people who desire to live in obedience to every word of God?

Who in your life might need the help of such a community in order to "get water from the well," and which gifts and abilities do you think God intends for you to contribute within such a community?

In what ways might God desire to bless you through such a community?

Memorize

Do good to your servant
*   according to your word, O Lord.*
Teach me knowledge and good judgment,
*   for I believe in your commands.*

Before I was afflicted I went astray,
*   but now I obey your word.*
You are good, and what you do is good;
*   teach me your decrees....*
It was good for me to be afflicted
*   so that I might learn your decrees.*
The law from your mouth is more precious to me
*   than thousands of pieces of silver and gold.*

Psalm 119:65 – 68, 71 – 72

NOT BY BREAD ALONE: MANNA AND WATER FROM THE ROCK

Exodus 16

After providing the Israelites with "twelve springs and seventy palm trees" at Elim (Exodus 15:27), God led them into the Desert of Sin. In contrast to the life they had known in Goshen, where rich soil and plentiful water produced food in abundance, this harsh wilderness challenged the Israelites' physical endurance. Their wilderness experience also challenged their perceptions and core beliefs about life and what it meant to live in relationship with their God.

One month after the Passover in Egypt, the Israelites faced another test in the sun-baked desert — another opportunity to demonstrate through obedient action what they really believed in their hearts. They became hungry — not just for the food they needed to sustain life, but for as much as they wanted of the kind of food they had eaten in Egypt — and they made their dissatisfaction known. As Psalm 78:18 records, "They willfully put God to the test by demanding the food they craved."

By his grace, God did not mete out punishment. Instead, he arranged for them to receive meat and bread — "enough" for each day. God's intent was to train his people to obey him and follow his instructions so that, by seeing how they lived, the whole world would come to know him. In order to fulfill their role as God's partners, the Israelites needed to leave behind every influence Egypt had on their hearts and lives. They needed to learn a new way of living. They not only needed to learn to obey God but *how* to obey him. They needed to become a unified, loving community that lived in total dependence on God's word, strength, and provision.

Would the Israelites trust in themselves — or in God? Would they rely on their qualifications — or on his? Would they live according to their ways — or by his ways? To reveal what was in their hearts, God soon allowed them to experience another water-related test at Rephidim.

As it turned out, the Israelites became angry and tested God! It seems that God's many miracles to free them from Egypt's bondage and his ever-present guidance and protection during the previous weeks didn't count for much. The Israelites said, in effect, "Unless you give us water, we won't follow you anymore. We're done being partners with you. Prove that you are really among us." So, at God's command, Moses walked all the way to Mount Sinai. Using his staff, Moses struck the mountain of God and water literally poured out to meet the needs of God's people.

But the crisis at Rephidim wasn't over. There were still lessons to be learned in order for these former slaves to become the redemptive community God intended them to be. An attack by the Amalekites on the vulnerable stragglers demonstrated that God's chosen people needed another lesson in building community. In this case, the Israelites responded to the crisis by trusting God and coming together to defeat the Amalekites.

Today God still trains his people. For those of us who will partner with him in restoring shalom to his creation, God provides experiences that will make us worthy of our calling. He will test us to know if we will obey and trust him completely, no matter how easy or difficult the way may be. Will we bring our needs before him, depend on him, and seize opportunities to demonstrate our full commitment to him when we face difficult and painful circumstances? During times of plenty, will we still remember him? When we don't feel our desperate need for his divine provision and protection, will we still be faithful to him? Will we still obey him and give him the glory for all that he has done and is doing for us?

Opening Thoughts (3 minutes)

The Very Words of God

> *Remember how the LORD your God led you all the way in the desert*
> *these forty years, to humble you and to test you in order to know what*
> *was in your heart, whether or not you would keep his commands.*
> *He humbled you, causing you to hunger and then feeding you with*
> *manna, which neither you nor your fathers had known, to teach you*
> *that man does not live on bread alone but on every word that comes*
> *from the mouth of the LORD.*

Deuteronomy 8:2 – 3

Think About It

When we experience difficult times that threaten our sense of
security, we are sometimes surprised by the beliefs and attitudes
that become evident under pressure. What kind of opportunities
does God give us to demonstrate what we really believe about life,
ourselves, and our relationship with him, and what impact do these
experiences have on our walk with him?

DVD Notes (33 minutes)

Test number two: hungry for what?

Will they obey and trust in "just enough"?

Training to be a community

Test number three: Rephidim

Their quarrel with Moses and God

Trained to be God's community

The hardest test of all

DVD Discussion (5 minutes)

1. On the map of Lower Egypt and the Sinai Peninsula, locate the Desert of Sin and Rephidim, and consider the desolate, rugged territory through which God had been leading the Israelites.

    Would you and your family have been willing to travel through this wilderness on foot carrying everything you

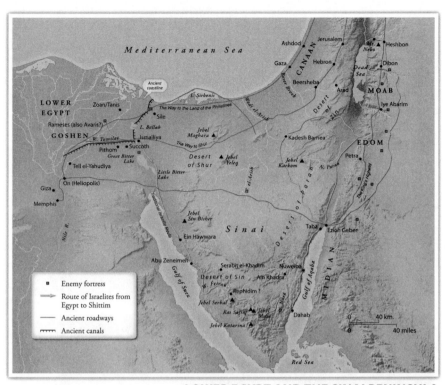

LOWER EGYPT AND THE SINAI PENINSULA

owned, not knowing where or when you would find food and water? Explain your answer.

To what extent might you have been a bit impatient with the way in which God was supplying your needs?

What are your thoughts about God's method for training his people in trust and dependence on him?

IMAGINE HOW SPENDING WEEKS TRAVELING THROUGH THIS VAST, INHOSPITABLE WILDERNESS WOULD CHALLENGE YOUR PERSPECTIVE ON WHAT IT MEANS TO BE A TRUSTING, OBEDIENT PARTNER WITH GOD.

How many "tests" might you and your faith community have needed in this setting in order to become the trusting, obedient, faithful community of partners God desired?

2. As weeks in this desert wilderness passed, in what ways did the Israelites demonstrate that they were "getting it" — that they were learning to faithfully obey and trust in God?

3. Why was the people's testing of God at Rephidim so serious, and what did it reveal about their hearts? Moses' heart? God's heart?

Small Group Bible Discovery and Discussion (13 minutes)

Two Perspectives on God's Training

God has a plan for bringing shalom, the order and harmony of his original creation, to a world that has been broken by the chaos of sin. What is so amazing about his plan is that he uses the very humans whose sin destroyed shalom to be his messengers, his instruments, and his partners in that restoration! But before God's people can bring his life-transforming message, love, and justice to the world, they need to be trained to become fit partners in God's work. For the former Hebrew slaves, God chose the desert — a harsh environment that was completely different from Egypt — to be their

training ground. God designed each day in the desert, each step
of the journey, each test to progressively take "Egypt" out of his
people.

1. What do you think God desired his people to discover about
    him as a result of their time in the desert wilderness? (See
    Exodus 16:4, 11 – 12; 17:10 – 13; Psalm 78:14 – 22.)

    The Israelites were stubborn and slow to listen to God and
    learn from him. Even so, how did he respond to them?

    In contrast, how did they respond to him?

2. What did the prophet Jeremiah say about how God viewed
    the Israelites' training in the desert? (See Jeremiah 2:2 – 3.)

    What does this image reveal about God's motivation for the
    time of desert testing, and what does it say to you about the
    depth of his love?

FOR GREATER UNDERSTANDING
Two Windows

We gain perspective into the exodus primarily through two "windows." Through one, we see how God's people sinned and failed while he remained faithful to them and his promises concerning them. This perspective warns us to learn from the Israelites' failures—just as they learned from their failures. The other "window" reveals insight into the Hebrews' intimate relationship with God and the joy of experiencing his presence and provision during even the most difficult circumstances. This perspective invites us to learn as the Hebrews learned—and to delight in the God who is always faithful.

3. Despite the Israelites' complaints and their ungrateful, fearful hearts, how did Moses summarize God's provision for them during their desert training? (See Deuteronomy 2:7.)

   To what would you attribute the difference between Moses' perspective and the Israelites' perspective?

   What does this say about how we view the testing God brings into our lives?

4. Which lesson from the Israelites' experience of testing in the desert is important for God's people today to take to heart? (See 1 Corinthians 10:1 – 6.)

THINK ABOUT IT
The Generation that Left Egypt: Failure or Success?

If we "fast forward" from this point in the Israelites' desert training, we discover that the generation that left Egypt eventually spent forty years training in the desert. They failed often, and God forgave them often. Yet it can take a long time to shape a people into being effective partners in God's plan. Those who had spent much of their lives in Egypt never became the people God needed to fulfill his plan in the Promised Land, so they died in the desert.

Some of us might view the generation that perished in the desert as a failure, but the children they reared were prepared to take the next steps in God's plan to redeem his world. The children of the Hebrew slaves were ready — not perfect, but ready — to bring God's way of living into the Promised Land. Sure, they still struggled to obey God, but they became the vessels through whom Messiah would come. So what do you think? Did the generation of former Hebrew slaves who died in the desert utterly fail, or were they a success because they raised up a generation of people who were ready to carry on God's plan?

Faith Lesson (5 minutes)

We all experience pain. The death of a loved one. Loss of employment. Serious illness. Financial hardship. Natural disaster. The list goes on. Yet as we face such pain we each have a crucial choice: to seize opportunities to demonstrate our trust in and obedience to God even when the outcome of our situation is unknown and risky, or to obstinately insist on pursuing life the way we want it to be.

The writer of Psalm 73 knew well the struggles we face. As you read the following verses, think of the ways in which it describes the Israelites during their time of testing in the desert wilderness.

> *When my heart was grieved*
> *and my spirit embittered,*
> *I was senseless and ignorant;*
> *I was a brute beast before you.*

Yet I am always with you;
　　you hold me by my right hand.
You guide me with your counsel,
　　and afterward you will take me into glory.
Whom have I in heaven but you?
　　And earth has nothing I desire besides you.
My flesh and my heart may fail,
　　but God is the strength of my heart
　　and my portion forever.
Those who are far from you will perish;
　　you destroy all who are unfaithful to you.
But as for me, it is good to be near God.
　　I have made the Sovereign Lord *my refuge;*
　　I will tell of all your deeds.

Psalm 73:21 – 28

Now think about how well it describes you when you face times of "desert testing."

1. When have the words "grieved" and "embittered" described your spirit?

2. What do you think of the times when you have been a "brute beast" before your God?

3. In what ways has God been faithful to walk with you through whatever testing you have faced?

4. What is the source of true hope and strength?

5. What choice(s) have you made to make God your refuge, and what do you tell other people about what God has done for you?

Closing (1 minute)

Read aloud together Psalm 73:26 – 28: "My flesh and my heart may fail, but God is the strength of my heart and my portion forever. Those who are far from you will perish; you destroy all who are unfaithful to you. But as for me, it is good to be near God. I have made the Sovereign LORD my refuge; I will tell of all your deeds."

Then pray together, asking God to forgive you for the times you have been disobedient and resisted or refused to allow him to shape you as a suitable partner in his work. Pray for an open heart that will receive his training during easy as well as tough times. Ask him to help you live by his every word and trust him for all that you need.

Memorize

My flesh and my heart may fail,
but God is the strength of my heart
and my portion forever.
Those who are far from you will perish;
you destroy all who are unfaithful to you.
But as for me, it is good to be near God.
I have made the Sovereign LORD my refuge;
I will tell of all your deeds.

Psalm 73:26 – 28

Tested and Trained to Be God's Message

In-Depth Personal Study Sessions

Day One | God Teaches New Lessons in New Ways

The Very Words of God

> *Your ways, O God, are holy.*
>> *What god is so great as our God?*
> *You are the God who performs miracles;*
>> *you display your power among the peoples.*
> *With your mighty arm you redeemed your people,*
>> *the descendants of Jacob and Joseph....*
> *You led your people like a flock*
>> *by the hand of Moses and Aaron.*
>
>> *Psalm 77:13 – 15, 20*

Bible Discovery

God Uses a New Approach in Teaching His People

When the Hebrew slaves cried out in Egypt, God put into motion a plan to free them, redeem them, take them as his own, and be their God. At first, he taught the Hebrews who he was through his awesome demonstrations of power against the gods of Egypt. Then, before the final plague, he asked them to participate in their training by taking the risky step of obeying his Passover commands. In the barren desert, he used a different approach: he gathered his chosen people as his own and, like a shepherd, led them day by day, providing for their every need and training them in his ways.

1. The devastating plagues that God inflicted on Egypt helped to teach both the Egyptians and the Hebrew slaves who he was. But the plagues were also God's response to the Egyptian's creation story and worldview that placed Pharaoh in God's rightful place. In a sense, the plagues shattered the

Egyptian perception that Pharaoh maintained order (*ma'at*) in the universe. Through the plagues, God systematically undid the harmony he had built into creation, and there was nothing Pharaoh could do to stop it.

a. As you read the following portions of Scripture, note the contrasts between how God taught the Egyptians who he was and how he taught the Israelites who he was.[1]

Text	What God "Undid" to Teach the Egyptians	What God Did to Teach the Israelites
Ex. 7:20–24; 15:23–25		
Ex. 9:23–25; 16:4, 14–18		
Ex. 10:13–15; 16:11–13		
Ex. 7:17–20; 17:5–6		

b. What do these examples of how God taught the Israelites say to you about how he viewed them and what he wanted them to know about himself?

2. What was the nature of God's relationship with the Israelites? (See Psalm 77:20; 78:52–53; 80:1; 95:6–7.)

How was that relationship reflected in the ways God taught them in the desert?

3. In contrast to what God did to the Egyptians, what did God promise to do for the Israelites if they listened to his voice and obeyed his commands? (See Exodus 15:25 – 26.)

What did God desire to teach the Israelites about himself by making this promise?

4. Whether God's training would come in the form of plague or blessing was to some degree dependent on the Israelites' obedience. (See 1 Corinthians 10:1 – 12.) Why is it important for us to study diligently and learn from the Israelites' experience?

DID YOU KNOW?
The Many Meanings of "Desert"

The Hebrew word translated "desert" (*midbar,* derived from the root *dbr*) carries a host of nuances that enrich our understanding of why God chose such harsh topography to be Israel's training ground. In the uninhabited desert — the shepherd's home — flocks grazed the meager pasture on the hills and by oases and edges of inhabited farmland.

Dabar also means "word," "speaking," and "speech." *Madbir* means "shepherd" or "leader." *Daberet* means "words." *Dibber* means "speaker." The

continued on next page . . .

connection between "shepherd" and "words" or "speaker" comes from the traditional practice of Middle Eastern shepherds who lead their sheep with words rather than by driving the sheep or using dogs to herd them. Even today, the singsong voices of shepherd girls can be heard as they lead their flocks across hillsides.

Dober means "pasture," which in the desert is meager. But a good shepherd still finds sufficient pasture to provide for a flock.

Debir means "sanctuary" or "inner chamber" (Holy of Holies). The shepherd finds safe haven for the flock during dust storms or at night, which likely provided the root meaning of *debir*.

The Jewish people have noted the rich meanings of *dbr*. The shepherd (*madbir*) leads the sheep in the desert (*midbar*) by speaking (*dibber*) words (*dabar*) to them, leading them to pasture (*dober*) and providing sanctuary (*debir*) during times of danger. Likewise, the leader of God's flock speaks words in order to lead people to sanctuary and pasture. So God, as Shepherd, trained his people in the desert to follow every word from his mouth as he led them to sanctuary and pasture.

Reflection

God's provision for his people in the desert wasn't designed just to keep them alive; it was also to teach them who he was. He wanted his people to know him as their loving Shepherd and to show their love for him by obeying all of his commands. By being obedient followers, they would become God's partners in restoring shalom and breaking down the alienation between all people and their Creator.

What are some ways in which God has taught you about himself through demonstrations of his awesome power, as he taught the Egyptians and Hebrews before he brought his people out of Egypt?

What did you learn?

What was the impact of this teaching on your life?

In what way(s) has God taught you about himself by being your Shepherd in the midst of difficult times in the desert?

What did you learn?

What was the impact of this teaching on your life?

Moses spoke God's words to the Israelites in the desert, and that same text speaks to those of us who desire to be God's partners today. Deuteronomy 4:9 and 10:12 speak of the responsibility those who have been taught by God have regarding what they have learned from him.

Which things do you need to make sure do not "slip from your heart," and how are you watching yourself to ensure that this does not happen?

What are you doing to teach the next generation what God has taught you, and what do you think is the most effective way to teach them?

What is your commitment to loving God, walking in all of his ways, and serving him with all your heart and soul, and what is that commitment requiring of you today?

Memorize

Show me your ways, O Lord,
*   teach me your paths;*
guide me in your truth and teach me,
*   for you are God my Savior,*
*   and my hope is in you all day long.*
Remember, O Lord, your great mercy and love,
*   for they are from of old.*
Remember not the sins of my youth
*   and my rebellious ways;*
according to your love remember me,
*   for you are good, O Lord.*

Psalm 25:4 – 7

Day Two | The Second Test

The Very Words of God

In the desert the whole community grumbled against Moses and Aaron. The Israelites said to them, "If only we had died by the Lord's hand in Egypt! There we sat around pots of meat and ate all the food we wanted, but you have brought us out into this desert to starve this entire assembly to death."

Exodus 16:2 – 3

Bible Discovery

A Craving for Egypt

After his people complained about the bitter water at Marah, God provided miraculously … and then blessed them with water in abundance at Elim. Later, the community of God's people moved on into the desert. One month after they had left their homes in Goshen, the Israelites realized how much they longed for the good food they had enjoyed while living in Egypt. The harsh desert environment was providing them with another test, another opportunity to show God what was in their hearts.

1. To refresh your memory of why God led his people into the desert, first read Deuteronomy 8:1 – 5 and then Exodus 16:1 – 4.

   a. How did the Israelites respond to the hunger they experienced in the Desert of Sin?

   b. What did their response reveal about the attitude of their hearts regarding their needs, their leaders, and their God?

   c. How well was God's plan working?

DID YOU KNOW?

God did not test his people only to assess the level of their obedience. His testing also provided opportunities for the Israelites to know experientially the level of their submission to his commands. God not only wanted to determine whether they were worthy to be his people, but he gave them experiences that would make them worthy. He was not only testing them in order to find out *if* they would obey him but to train them so they would learn *how* to obey him. (See Deuteronomy 8:3.)

2. What was the Israelites' complaint? (See Exodus 16:2 – 3, Psalm 78:18 – 19.)

    What does the nature of their complaint reveal about the influence Egypt still had in their minds and hearts?

    What does the object of their complaint indicate about where they were placing their trust for provision?

3. How did Moses instruct the Israelites in order to correct their misconception about who was leading them, and why was this clarification important for them to understand? (See Exodus 16:6 – 8.)

4. What did God do that reinforced Moses' instruction and would help the people know him? (See Exodus 16:9 – 12.)

What impact would you have expected God's dramatic revelation of himself in the desert to have had on the Israelites?

What motivated God's revelation, and what impact did it appear to have had on his chosen people?

As you consider this interaction between God and his people, what do you realize about your own awareness of and sensitivity to God's desire to provide for your needs and reveal himself to you?

DID YOU KNOW?

When the Hebrews first saw the bread from heaven (Exodus 16:15), they asked "What is it?" Later they named it *manna* (Exodus 16:31). In Hebrew *man hu* can mean "what is it" or "it is manna." Thus the name is a clever pun not recognizable in English. Someone seeing manna for the first time might say "*man hu*?" (What is it?) The answer would be "*man hu*" (It is manna.)

5. How do we know that the crisis about food was really a faith crisis — a test of the Israelites' hearts? (See Exodus 16:13 - 30; Psalm 78:12 - 29.)

How would you describe the way God met the Israelites' need for food, and what does it reveal about his love for them and desire to bless them?

What about the experience of gathering manna helped the Israelites know and trust God and taught them to depend on him (and only him) to meet all of their needs?

What commands were the Israelites to obey for gathering manna, and what does God's response to their disobedience reveal about his purpose for the manna experience?

What values was God training into the hearts of the Israelites by teaching them how much manna they were to gather and when they were (and were not) to gather it?

DID YOU KNOW?

Through the gathering of manna, God began training his people to keep the Sabbath holy even before he gave them the Sabbath laws. By gathering the manna six days a week, the Israelites experienced, and thereby knew, the sacredness of the Sabbath. Jewish sages have noted that the Sabbath rest was not just for God's people. God also keeps the Sabbath sacred and rests from his work (Genesis 2:3). God would not send bread on the Sabbath because it was also a sacred day for him![2]

Reflection

The Israelites needed to know God experientially through his daily, sustaining provision, and they needed to learn to have trusting, obedient hearts toward him. We are no different. We also need to know God experientially and learn to love him with all our heart, soul, and strength. And we need to demonstrate that love by faithful obedience to his commands.

> The desert was God's chosen training ground for the Israelites. What has been (or is) God's training ground in your life so that you can *know* him and not just *know about* him?

> How has he provided for you during times of testing?

> What has he done to train you to trust and obey him?

How sensitive and responsive have you been to become a partner he loves, one who desires to participate in his plan of redemption?

When has a "food crisis," your inability to provide what you desperately needed in circumstances beyond your control, become for you a "faith crisis" during which you questioned God's provision, decisions, and love?

How did God respond to both your physical and your spiritual crises?

What did you learn as a result, and how did it change how you live?

Whether we recognize it or not, God provides for the daily physical needs of every person on earth — food to eat, air to breathe, water to drink, protection from disease. How willing are you to:

humbly recognize his gracious daily provision?

acknowledge your daily dependence on him?

respond with a thankful, obedient heart?

In a culture in which we are inclined to depend on our own strength and protect ourselves against every loss — through insurance policies, retirement funds, extra food stored away — how easy is it to forget how dependent you are on God's daily provision?

In contrast, how does recognizing your dependence on God for your daily needs deepen your trust in him in all areas of life?

What specific things do you do to remind yourself of God's provision?

God commanded Moses to keep a jar of manna as a reminder of his faithful provision for his people during their desert training (Exodus 16:32 – 35). Some people today will place in their yard a large stone or stones (reminiscent of the standing stones mentioned in Exodus 24:4 and Joshua 4:4 – 9) as a reminder of God's faithful provision and training. What active steps might you take to remind yourself (and to testify to others such as children, grandchildren, and anyone who might ask) of God's faithfulness and sustaining care?

FOR GREATER UNDERSTANDING
Jesus and the Bread from Heaven

God's provision of manna, the "bread from heaven," was a crucial element in his training of his people for their future role in the Promised Land. And Moses was God's instrument to provide it (Exodus 16:4). For generations, these events have remained a central theme in the spiritual heritage of the Jewish people.

Part of that heritage included the promise that God would send another prophet, the Messiah, who would be humble like Moses and speak to God's people (Deuteronomy 18:15–18). The Jewish people of Jesus' day were well schooled in all the teachings of the Torah. So when Jesus described himself as one who was "gentle and humble in heart" (Matthew 11:29), he immediately caught their attention because that is what Moses was like. And when Jesus miraculously fed the five thousand with bread, some began to think that he was, indeed, this promised Moses-like prophet (John 6:1–14). They talked with Jesus about the bread from heaven that God provided in the desert, and Jesus told them that he was the bread from heaven who would give life to the world! (John 6:25–36, 48–51)

Although most did not believe Jesus was who he claimed to be, try to imagine what a thrill it must have been for those who did believe to see how God was acting to fulfill the promises he made to his people during Israel's desert experience. As their eyes were opened to God's amazing work among his people from generation to generation, imagine how they came to know — *experience* — God in their hearts. No wonder his disciples were so motivated to live for him and show others who he was!

Day Three | Becoming the Community of God

The Very Words of God

> *Jacob said to Joseph, "God Almighty appeared to me at Luz in the land*
> *of Canaan, and there he blessed me and said to me, 'I am going to*
> *make you fruitful and will increase your numbers. I will make you*
> *a community of peoples, and I will give this land as an everlasting*
> *possession to your descendants after you.'"*

Genesis 48:3 – 4

Bible Discovery

Trained to Be the Community of God

For a time, the ancient Hebrews lived as an enslaved people in a foreign land, but God had bigger plans for them. He not only wanted them to be his people by race, he wanted them to function as a community of people who loved him with all their heart and showed the world who he was by the way they loved him and cared for one another. The making of such a community wasn't easy, however. For the Israelites, it required step-by-step training in facing the difficult challenges that forge community.

1. Imagine the scene when God sweetened the water at Marah. How would it have been possible for thousands of Israelites, who had not found water for three days, to obtain water from one well? (See Exodus 15:22 – 26.)

   What "decree" and "law" might God have given to help them during this process?

2. One month after they had left Egypt, how does the text
    describe the Israelites? (See Exodus 16:1 – 2.)

    Although they are starting to pull together as a community,
    what indicates that they need still more training?

3. What specific instructions did God give regarding the gath-
    ering of manna? (See Exodus 16:16 – 21.)

    In what way(s) did these instructions build community by
    encouraging an awareness of the needs of others and one's
    responsibility to gather no more than required?

4. The next test for the Israelites came at Rephidim, where
    there was no water (Exodus 17:1 – 7). The text refers, as
    it did when the Israelites complained about their food in
    the Desert of Sin, to "the whole Israelite community." But
    their complaint (Exodus 17:3) in the Hebrew text is literally
    translated in the singular: "Why did you bring *me* up out of
    Egypt to make *me* and my children and [*my*] livestock die
    of thirst?" Although the Israelites are becoming more like a
    community in some ways, what does their complaint reveal
    about the true focus of their hearts?

5. When God sent Moses to strike the rock at Horeb in order to obtain water, who did God say to take with him? (See Exodus 17:5 – 6.)

Why might God have wanted these particular people to be eyewitnesses of what he would do?

DID YOU KNOW?

According to Jewish sages, the three tests on the journey to Sinai (bitter water at Marah, manna in the Desert of Sin, no water at Rephidim) all focus on learning three things: (1) total trust in God, (2) total trust in Moses, and (3) how to be a caring and unified community. It is interesting that the Torah uses a plural pronoun to describe the Israelites during their journey from Egypt to Mount Sinai. But when they arrive at Mount Sinai, the singular pronoun is used, indicating that they have become a united people, a caring community.

Reflection

Immediately after the Israelites tested God at Rephidim, Amalekites attacked the stragglers of the community who had lagged behind (Exodus 17:8, Deuteronomy 25:17 – 18). Apparently the community of God's people had not come together enough to protect and help the weak, tired, and helpless among them.

What message do you take to heart from this tragedy?

To what extent are you reaching out to lift up others who are experiencing difficult times — illness, injury, or infirmity; financial crisis; family disunity or stress; injustice, and so on?

To what extent are you so consumed by your own needs and crises that you "hoard" your resources (financial, time, emotional, and spiritual) and push the needs of other people from your attention?

Being a community, of course, reaches far beyond our individual attitudes and actions. What responsibility does the faith community of Jesus have to reach out and provide practical help and a message of hope to those who are weak, hurting, and struggling?

To what extent is the maturity of a faith community revealed by whether or not the hurting and weak are protected in the middle of the community or are pushed to the outskirts where they are most vulnerable?

What about your faith community? In what ways has it been tested by difficult challenges, and what were the results?

To what extent is the community caring for the weak and hurting, and what improvements need to be made?

If you value participation in God's community enough to not only find it but to contribute to it, what would be a good next step for you to take toward becoming the kind of faith community God desires?

Memorize

May the God who gives endurance and encouragement give you a spirit of unity among yourselves as you follow Christ Jesus, so that with one heart and mouth you may glorify the God and Father of our Lord Jesus Christ.

Romans 15:5 – 6

Day Four | The Third Test: No Water

The Very Words of God

[Moses] called the place Massah and Meribah because the Israelites quarreled and because they tested the Lord *saying, "Is the* Lord *among us or not?"*

Exodus 17:7

Bible Discovery

The Hebrews Test God!

God gave the Israelites a third test during their desert training. This time, their lack of community was more obvious and their lack of trust more defiant. In fact, this time the people actually *tested God*!

1. What happened when God led his people to Rephidim? (See Exodus 17:1 – 3.)

   Why had God brought them to a place of suffering and need again? (See Deuteronomy 8:1 – 5.)

   What insight does Psalm 81:7 – 11 provide as to God's intent in leading the Israelites to Rephidim and what he wanted them to know about him? (Remember, "know" means to know experientially as well as intellectually.)

   Did God really want them to be without water? How do you know?

   What perspective does this give you into understanding the hearts of the Israelites and their lack of trust in the heart of God?

2. How does God respond when people "put him to the test" and treat him with contempt by demanding that he demonstrate his power and provision *before* they trust him — thus casting doubt on his ability and his character? (See Deuteronomy 6:16; Numbers 14:20 – 23; Psalm 95:8 – 10.)

3. In what way(s) did the Israelites' quarrel with Moses (and by extension, God) at Rephidim differ from their previous complaints? (See Exodus 15:24; 16:2; 17:1 – 7.)

How did Moses respond to the Israelites' anger and defiance?

In what way was God's answer to Moses also an answer to the Israelites' arrogant questioning of the motive of God's heart and his presence with them?

MOSES NEEDS HELP!

Moses had cried out to God before, but this time was different—he feared for his life! The Hebrew word used here, *ze'akah*, means "a passionate and loud cry of pain." God responds to such cries, and there is much we can learn from how he responds.

In this case, God told Moses to go and stand in front of the very people whom Moses feared would stone him! There is a bit of humor in God's response, but think of what God was teaching through these instructions. Moses also needed to know experientially that God was his ever-present protector. Wouldn't God's protection of Moses before an angry, threatening congregation prove that God was indeed among them?

4. Despite the insolence of the Israelites and the abuse they were heaping on God and his servant Moses, what was God going to do for his people? (See Exodus 17:5 – 6.)

FOR GREATER UNDERSTANDING

God Sent Moses to Horeb

God sent Moses to Horeb to strike the rock (or cliff) of the mountain with the staff of God, the same staff Moses had used to demonstrate God's power and to bring about the deliverance of the Hebrews from Egypt. God promised that when Moses struck the rock, water for God's people would run out from the mountain and into the desert.

THESE ARE THE "TRADITIONAL" SINAI MOUNTAINS. WHETHER OR NOT ONE OF THESE IS THE ACTUAL MOUNT SINAI OF THE EXODUS, THE SCENE PROVIDES A SENSE OF THE RUGGED GRANDEUR OF THE DESERT MOUNTAINS WHERE GOD LED THE ISRAELITES. THINK ABOUT MOSES, WHO TRAVELED THROUGH MOUNTAINS LIKE THESE TO BRING LIFE-GIVING WATER TO THE ISRAELITES.

We don't know exactly where that mountain is or how far it was from the Israelites' encampment (the exact location of which is also uncertain). Scholars generally agree, however, that Horeb and Mount Sinai refer to the same general location. Some scholars think that Horeb, which means "dry," is a more general word for the area and that Sinai is the name of the specific mountain on which God chose to appear. Others scholars believe Horeb and Mount Sinai are different words for the same place.

The mountain Moses struck, whether called Horeb or Mount Sinai, is also referred to as the "mountain of God" because to the Israelites it symbolized God's holy presence. So when water came from the "rock," God clearly was its source.

What (and who) did God tell Moses to take with him to Horeb?

Why do you think God specified that these representatives of his power and his people go with Moses?

Reflection

When we face difficulties, it is all too easy to test God and make our belief in him conditional on a demonstration of his power. We may demand that God prove his love for us and his presence with us by solving our difficulties before we will obey him. But those who would partner with God cannot hold on to such attitudes of distrust. To do so is to hold God in contempt as the Israelites did at Rephidim. Those who would partner with God must take courage and walk humbly in obedience to his word.

In which area(s) of your life might you be testing God and subtly expecting him to prove himself by rescuing you?

For example, what if:

- You eat an unhealthy diet, then ask God to heal you when you experience health issues?
- You barely open a textbook all semester but ask God to help you get a good grade anyway?
- You practice unsafe driving habits but ask God to protect you as you drive?
- You take shortcuts and do as little as possible at work but still pray for a promotion and a pay raise?
- You engage in high-risk hobbies and expect God's protection?

These — and many other behaviors and attitudes — subtly demand that God provide for you even though you may not be fully committed to obeying his will. What changes in your lifestyle, behaviors, or attitudes might you need to make in order to approach God with a humble heart as you seek his provision and protection?

At one time or another, most of us reach a point at which we truly wonder if God is with us, if he is still our protector and provider. How can we ask the question, "Where are you, God?" with humility and an obedient heart rather than with contempt? Take some time to study Psalm 31:1 – 3 below and focus your thoughts on obedient ways to ask God to demonstrate his presence and power:

> *In you, O Lord, I have taken refuge;*
>> *let me never be put to shame;*
>> *deliver me in your righteousness.*
> *Turn your ear to me,*
>> *come quickly to my rescue;*
> *be my rock of refuge,*
>> *a strong fortress to save me.*
> *Since you are my rock and my fortress,*
>> *for the sake of your name lead and guide me.*

What differences do you see in the psalmist's attitude toward God as opposed to the attitude of the Israelites at Rephidim?

What do you think is the motivation of the psalmist's heart?

How would you describe the kind of relationship the psalmist seems to have with God?

How, on the basis of what you know experientially of God and the relationship you have with him, might you ask him to show himself to you or act on your behalf during a time of need or suffering?

DID YOU KNOW?

Some scholars have noted that the image of Moses striking the mountain of God (also Horeb or Mount Sinai) is a picture of God's willingness to be struck as though he were receiving the punishment—the blow of the staff—that the Hebrews deserved. This image also portrays God as the source of the life-giving water he was providing for the Israelites. If so, Moses striking the rock at Horeb is an early "picture" of the ministry of Jesus, who would bear the punishment for sin and pour out his life to give life to the world. God displayed no anger toward the Hebrews at this time, but later they learned about his anger.

WHEN ISRAEL CAME TO THE WILDERNESS OF SIN, THEIR WATER RAN OUT. INSTEAD OF TRUSTING GOD, THEY COMPLAINED BITTERLY, BUT THE LORD FORGAVE THEM AND SENT MOSES TO THE MOUNTAIN OF GOD SOME DISTANCE AWAY. THERE, AS GOD "STOOD" ON THE ROCK, MOSES STRUCK IT AND WATER GUSHED OUT OF IT. WATER FLOWED DOWN THE MOUNTAIN AND INTO THE DESERT WHERE THE PEOPLE WERE ENCAMPED. THE ISRAELITES RECEIVED GOD'S PROVISION OF WATER IN SPITE OF THEIR REBELLION, BUT BECAUSE OF THEIR STUBBORN REFUSAL TO TRUST GOD, THEY MISSED OUT ON THE BLESSING OF SEEING THE MIRACLE OF THE WATER COME FROM THE ROCK.

Day Five | Moses' Example of Faithful Obedience

The Very Words of God

> *Moses cried out to the LORD, "What am I to do with these people? They are almost ready to stone me."*
>
> *The LORD answered Moses, "Walk on ahead of the people. Take with you some of the elders of Israel and take in your hand the staff with which you struck the Nile, and go. I will stand there before you by the rock at Horeb. Strike the rock, and water will come out of it for the people to drink." So Moses did this in the sight of the elders of Israel.*
>
> *Exodus 17:4 – 6*

Bible Discovery

Obeying at All Costs

Imagine how Moses felt when the Hebrews quarreled with him again — this time with more anger than ever before — when a serious difficulty arose at Rephidim. After all that God had done for them during their relatively brief walk with him, they not only tested God by demanding that he prove himself to them, they thought of returning to Egypt and threatened to kill Moses! How might you have responded if you were in Moses' sandals?

1. What was Moses' source of guidance as he led the Israelites through the desert, and what does this reveal about his motivation as a leader? (See Exodus 17:1.)

2. Although Moses feared for his life when the Israelites rebelled defiantly at Rephidim, notice how he responded to

them as the shepherd whom God had chosen to lead them.
(See Exodus 17:2 – 6.)

    a.   What did Moses say to the people?

    b.   What did Moses say to God?

    c.   What did God say to Moses?

    d.   What did Moses do?

    e.   What did Moses' response reveal about his commitment
        to do whatever God told him to do?

3.   How does Moses' role as described in Psalm 99:6 – 7 com-
    pare with the role God desired his people, Israel, to have in
    the world? (See Exodus 19:3 – 6.)

    Would you agree that Moses fulfilled the roles of a priest
    well — keeping the laws of God's covenant and mediating
    between God and the people (bringing their concerns to
    God and revealing God's desires to them)? Why or why not?

What kind of an example, then, is Moses for followers of Christ today who are also called to be a kingdom of priests in service to God? (See Revelation 1:6.)

FOR GREATER UNDERSTANDING
Moses Matures as God's Chosen Leader

Moses is undoubtedly one of the great people of God in the Bible, one of few who frequently conversed with God person to person. But we may tend to think of Moses as a person unlike ourselves, as one who "always had it together" in his relationship with God. The insight of the Jewish sages, however, softens the unattainable, bigger-than-life image we may have of Moses. They see in the life of Moses a series of confrontations—up to the end of his life—through which he demonstrated significant maturing in his trust in God. Consider, for example, these confrontations:

- Between Moses and God (Exodus 3–4)
- Between Moses and Pharaoh (Exodus 5, 7–11)
- Between Moses and Israel (Exodus 15:22–17:15; 32–33; Numbers 11–14; 20)

Over time, how did Moses change in terms of his trust in God's faithfulness, his obedience to God's commands, his leadership of God's people, and his vulnerability in his personal relationship with God? In what ways does Moses' growth in maturity before God encourage you in your commitment to walk with God?

Reflection

During the test at Rephidim, as in all the tests before and all that were to come, Moses could have responded differently. He could have petitioned God to choose a new leader, argued long and hard with Israel's elders about what to do, made his own plan, battled God over the need for another painful training experience, or just plain quit. Instead, he called on God and responded as God commanded. As a result, he matured in his faith and stands even today as an example of how to learn God's ways and walk in faithful obedience before him.

Moses also knew that the tests of hardship in the desert weren't the only or necessarily the most difficult ones that God's people would face. He repeatedly warned them that when their needs were met and life was good to "be careful that you do not forget the LORD" (Deuteronomy 6:10 – 13; 8:10 – 14, 19.) This, perhaps, is the most difficult test of all.

When you feel the pressure of testing, what are you inclined to do?

In what ways is it difficult for you to cry out to God (and do so without contempt)?

How hard is it for you to obey God, especially when obedience seems to make your path even more difficult (such as God's instruction to Moses to "walk to Horeb")?

When things are going well for you and your basic needs are met, how easy is it for you to focus on your desires and forget about the Lord?

Is your need to seek God and obey him fully any less important when life is good as opposed to when it is difficult? Why or why not?

In what way(s) might God be testing your commitment to obey him at all costs — even during the good times?

When life is good, which of God's commands do you find difficult to obey?

What might be the consequences of your disobedience in these areas — for you, your family, your faith community, your world?

Memorize

Moses said to the LORD *... "You have said, 'I know you by name and you have found favor with me.' If you are pleased with me, teach me your ways so I may know you and continue to find favor with you. Remember that this nation is your people."*

Exodus 33:12 – 13

THEIR BLOOD CRIED OUT: ISRAEL BECOMES A COMMUNITY

Exodus 17:8–16

God's love for humankind is amazing. He displays great mercy in molding and shaping people to be partners in his work of restoring shalom to a world that has been broken by chaos. With patience and longsuffering, he seems to delight in using the weaknesses of unlikely people to bring glory to his name. So God chose the Hebrew people to become a nation, a community of people who would reveal his shalom to the world.

There was a problem, however. The Hebrews were cruelly enslaved by the Egyptians. They cried out in pain, and God heard their anguished cry. He sent Moses to deliver them, but Pharaoh would not let his slaves go to worship their God. That was a situation with which God has absolutely no patience and to which he responded with frightening fury. When someone obstructs the work of God's kingdom; causes suffering among the weak, poor, or defenseless; or prevents the needy from experiencing his shalom, God hears their cry and his anger knows no bounds.

As the Hebrews watched from the sidelines, God responded to their situation by sending the first nine plagues on Egypt. Then, before the angel of death passed over to kill Egypt's firstborn, God called the Hebrews into action. God commanded the whole community of his people to put lambs' blood on their doorposts, get ready to leave in a hurry, prepare a special meal, and wait for the appointed time. They obeyed, and soon marched out into the desert, following Moses and the cloud of God to the Red Sea. There, God miraculously parted the sea and enabled all of them to cross it on dry land. Only when they were safe on the other side did the wrath of his anger destroy the army of Pharaoh.

As a people, the Hebrews, the new nation of Israel, danced together on the other side of the sea, rejoicing in their God and his awesome power and love. They seemed to be a community, and in some ways they were, but they had much to learn about being the community through which God would bring his shalom to the world and demonstrate his character to the nations. They still carried within their hearts much of Egypt's darkness — in self-serving actions and attitudes. At times they became so self-centered, so individualistic, so determined to meet their own needs that they stopped protecting and caring for the weak and needy among them.

The focus of our study begins, as do so many stories in the Hebrew text, with trouble: "The Amalekites came and attacked the Israelites" (Exodus 17:8), those who were weak and had lagged behind. We will consider how God used the Amalekites — fierce desert nomads and slave traders — to remind the Israelites of his love for the weak and weary, disadvantaged and sick, poor and needy. We will see how God used that situation to train them in how to be *his* community of people.

In our modern world where many people suffer, where the chaos of sin and selfish pursuits frequently seem to overshadow God's purpose, we should take to heart what Israel learned about God and his desire for them to become a community of faithful partners in bringing shalom to the world. Their experiences teach us about the heart of God: his deep love and concern for weak and suffering people, and his fury against those who seek to frustrate his unfolding redemptive purpose. God will always hear the cry — the *ze'akah* — of those who suffer under the brutality of chaos. And he will often call on the community of his people to be his partners in restoring shalom. The question is, are we the community he has called us to be?

Opening Thoughts (3 minutes)

The Very Words of God

> All kings will bow down to him
>   and all nations will serve him.
> For he will deliver the needy who cry out,
>   the afflicted who have no one to help.
> He will take pity on the weak and the needy
>   and save the needy from death.
> He will rescue them from oppression and violence,
>   for precious is their blood in his sight.
>
> *Psalm 72:11 – 14*

Think About It

Those of us who seek to walk with God know that we are responsible to offer help and hope to those who are weak, poor, or defenseless. For us to participate in the oppression of those who are less fortunate is unthinkable.

But how much thought do we really give to the weak, needy, and vulnerable? They live in our communities, our country, and in every other nation on earth — they even worship in our faith communities — but do we know who they are? Do we know them well enough to recognize them, identify their needs, and offer assistance? If our busy, self-serving lifestyles dull our awareness to others in need, in what ways might we actually be contributing to their oppression?

DVD Notes (29 minutes)

God hears the cry of hurting people

The Amalekites attack

Israel prepares for battle

Moses raises his "stick"—symbol of God's power

***Adonai* is our "banner"**

Who hears *ze'akah*?

DVD Discussion (6 minutes)

1.   By the time they reached Rephidim, the Israelites had traveled in the desert for about six weeks. On the map of Lower Egypt and the Sinai Peninsula, locate the Desert of Sin, Rephidim, and Jebel Katarina and Jebel Musa.

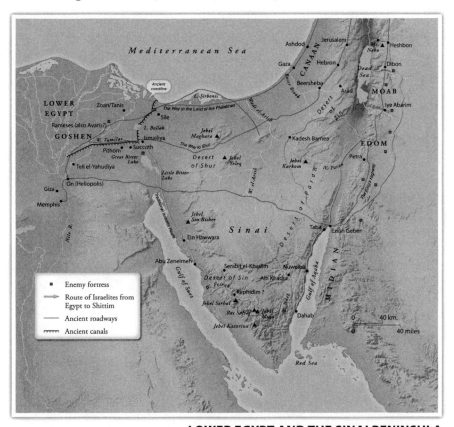

LOWER EGYPT AND THE SINAI PENINSULA

From the video images you have seen, you have an idea of how vast, rugged, and desolate the deserts of Sinai are. Try to imagine yourself as an Israelite. No matter which route you traveled toward Mount Sinai (and no matter which mountain Mount Sinai actually is), the flowing waters and green fields of Goshen are now far behind you. Now let your imagination go a step further and picture yourself as one of Israel's stragglers — thirsty and perhaps feeling forgotten by God, weary and having been abandoned by your fellow travelers.

What do you think it would have been like to be in that condition in that place and to be attacked by the Amalekites, who were hardened desert nomads known for their raiding parties and slave trading? Would God have heard *ze'akah* from you?

2. Do you think the Israelites viewed it as mere coincidence that while they were longing for the "good life" in Egypt, the Amalekites (who most likely would take them back there as slaves) attacked? Why or why not?

3. How would you describe the breakdown of the Israelite community before the Amalekites attacked in comparison to the building up of that community as the Israelites responded to the attack?

4. As the Israelites saw Moses, with the help of Aaron and Hur raising the "stick" of God on top of the hill, what do you think the image reminded them of, and in what ways might they have come to *know* their God as never before?

5. Why is it important for people who live for God to always hear (and respond to) the *ze'akah* cry?

Small Group Bible Discovery and Discussion (16 minutes)

God Responds to Cries of Ze'akah

Ze'akah, one of the most impassioned, power-filled words in Hebrew, communicates intense emotion. Usually translated as "cry" or "outcry," the depth of suffering that causes such a cry is not conveyed by English words. *Ze'akah* implies a heart-wrenching wailing; though there are no recognizable words, when you hear it you know what it is. Such an outcry rises out of great pain, suffering, and despair caused not simply by impersonal suffering but by the brutality and cruelty of other people. Scripture reveals that God never fails to hear *ze'akah*, and his response against those who cause it is frightening.

1. Genesis 4:1 – 12 is the first recorded *ze'akah* in the Bible. Who caused it, and what was his response to what he had done?

   In contrast, what did God hear, and how did he respond to the cry?

   What did Jesus say about people who shed the innocent blood of the righteous? (See Matthew 23:33 – 36.)

   In what ways do the responses of God and his Son, Jesus, give you a better picture of what the writers of the text understood *ze'akah* to mean?

DID YOU KNOW?

Nahum Sarna, the great Exodus scholar, notes, "[*Ze'akah*] is one of the most powerful words in the language. Pervaded by moral outrage and soul-stirring passion, it denotes the anguished cry of the oppressed, the agonized plea of the helpless victim."[1]

2. Genesis 18 and 19 record the story of the cry that went up to God from Sodom and Gomorrah.

   a. How did God respond to that cry? (See Genesis 18:20 – 21; 19:1 – 13, 24 – 25.)

   b. There is no mistaking that the immorality and sexual perversion of those cities offended God, but later prophets add to our understanding of the nature of the *ze'akah* that went up to God. What was taking place in those cities that would have brought harm to the righteous, the weak, and the defenseless? (See Isaiah 1:10, 15 – 17.)

   c. What insight do you gain from Isaiah and Genesis 18:23 and 19:27 – 29 as to the reason for the severity of God's response? What is God concerned about preventing and preserving?

3. Exodus records the story of the Hebrews' suffering and departure from Egypt. Who had caused the Hebrews' *ze'akah* — their cry of agonized suffering — and what effect did their cry have on God? (See Exodus 1:8 – 11; 2:23 – 25; 3:7 – 10.)

4.* What insight do you gain into God's passionate concern for
the oppressed and his fury at their oppressors from the cry
of *ze'akah* lifted up in Exodus 11:1 – 6 and 12:29 – 30?

5. When God gave his laws to Israel, he clearly stated what will
happen to one who causes *ze'akah* by taking advantage of
one who is weaker. What do these commands reveal to you
about the heart of God and what he values in the hearts of
those who follow him? (See Exodus 22:21 – 27.)

THINK ABOUT IT
God Still Responds to Ze'akah; Will You?

We would do well to remember how much God's great heart beats with compassion for those who are suffering. His anger still burns against the people
or culture that causes or contributes to suffering. People in our increasingly
Hellenistic (humanistic) society are so focused on their own well-being, interests, success, and comfort that their concern for the oppressed and suffering
is diminishing. Yet even if no one else is listening, God still hears the *ze'akah*
of injustice, and he will respond. His wrath against those who cause it knows
no bounds.

Remember too that God partners with people to provide help and hope to
the weak and suffering. After hearing the enslaved Hebrews' cry in Egypt, he
chose Moses and Aaron to be "as God to Pharaoh" and rescue the Hebrews
by his power. When the Amalekites attacked, God used Moses, Aaron, Hur,
and Joshua to help Israel defeat those who caused an outcry of *ze'akah*.
Throughout the Torah, Historical Books, and Prophets, writers of the text
challenged God's people to be concerned for those who suffer and to respond
in righteousness, justice, and love because at one time they were "slaves in
Egypt" and knew what it was to suffer.

During the days he walked the earth, Jesus showed great compassion to those who suffered. He commanded his disciples to feed the hungry, visit the lonely and the prisoner, and clothe the naked because to do this was (and still is!) to do it for him. Those of us who seek to walk as Jesus walked are still God's privileged partners in bringing shalom to the chaos around us. Having experienced the shalom that Jesus provides to all who believe in him, we now are to share it with hurting people in every way we can.

Faith Lesson (5 minutes)

If we claim to live for God — to walk as Jesus walked (1 John 2:6) — we must demonstrate our love for God by obeying his commandments. This includes listening for the cry of the broken-hearted, the needy, the suffering, the poor, the unborn, the persecuted, and the sick, and then responding with the justice and compassion that represents the heart of God.

1. Long after God's people had settled in the Promised Land, part of God's complaint against them was that they worshiped him with their lips and offerings and yet, like Sodom and Gomorrah, they had blood on their hands from injustice, oppression, and evil deeds against the defenseless (Isaiah 1:10 – 17). Using Sodom as an example, the prophet Ezekiel also warned God's people about their "detestable" deeds and being "arrogant, overfed, and unconcerned" about the poor and needy (Ezekiel 16:49 – 50).

   In what ways are God's people today guilty of the same offenses:

   - Injustice?
   - Oppression?
   - Evil deeds?
   - Arrogance?
   - Being overfed?
   - Unconcerned?

In what specific ways are you guilty?

2. Proverbs 21:13 warns against shutting our ears to the cries of the poor and needy — the cries that God always hears.

   a. To what extent are you listening (and responding) to the cries of the poor, the forgotten elderly, the unborn, the orphans, those who are persecuted, the unemployed, the sick, and the exploited?

   b. Do you think it makes any difference to God whether you choose not to help or simply don't help because of apathy? Why or why not?

3. If your ears are open, what action does the cry of *ze'akah* prompt you to take on behalf of someone who is needy or hurting?

Closing (1 minute)

Read Psalm 22:23 – 24 aloud together: "You who fear the LORD, praise him! . . . For he has not despised or disdained the suffering of the afflicted one; he has not hidden his face from him but has listened to his cry for help."

Then pray together, thanking God for his mercy and faithfulness in hearing the cries of the oppressed, the weak, and the needy. Ask him to make you more sensitive to the needs of these people, especially those in your own community, and more aware of opportunities to provide help and hope. Thank him for his willingness to use you as his partner, and ask him to nurture within you a compassionate, generous heart that is more like his.

Memorize

You who fear the Lord, praise him!...
For he has not despised or disdained
*   the suffering of the afflicted one;*
he has not hidden his face from him
*   but has listened to his cry for help.*

Psalm 22:23 – 24

Tested and Trained to Be God's Message

In-Depth Personal Study Sessions

Day One | Who Were the Amalekites?

The Very Words of God

> *I will completely blot out the memory of Amalek from under heaven.*
>
> **Exodus 17:14**

Bible Discovery

Bitter Enemies of God and His People

The nomadic Amalekites lived in the deserts south of the Promised Land and were bitter enemies of God's people. Apparently slave traders, they are not mentioned in any writings other than the Bible, and no archaeological information exists for them. Jewish tradition speaks often of Amalekites being perpetual enemies of God's people. Because of their treachery against the most vulnerable of the Israelites, *Amalek* became the descriptive term for various eternal enemies of God's people who sought Israel's destruction in order to frustrate the purposes of God.

1. As the Israelites approached Mount Sinai, they entered Amalekite territory. Why do you think the Amalekites, who had a reputation for extreme brutality and no conscience, attacked the weary and weak people who had lagged behind rather than attacking the main encampment? (See Deuteronomy 25:17 – 19.)

DATA FILE

Amalekites: Descendants of Esau

The roots of the bitter conflict between Esau and his twin brother, Jacob (renamed Israel), went deep, which helps to explain why the Amalekites, descendants of Esau, were utterly determined to destroy God's people (Genesis 25:21–26; 26:34–35; 27:36–41; 36:6–8; Numbers 24:17–18.)

Esau had twelve sons who founded the twelve tribes comprising Esau's descendants, the Edomites (Genesis 36:9–19).[2] Amalek, son of Timna (a concubine of Esau's son, Eliphaz), belatedly became the "thirteenth" tribe. Because his mother was not a full wife, Amalek was a lesser son, making the Amalekites a lesser tribe of the Edomites. Timna was a Horite, a people indigenous to Mount Seir, but the Edomites displaced the Horites, who became desert nomads (Deuteronomy 2:12). The Amalekites also were displaced and had become a significant nomadic tribe by the time the Israelites encountered them in the region of Mount Sinai.

2. Even though, as Jewish thought holds, God seems to have allowed the Amalekites to attack in order to discipline the Israelites for their lack of trust and lack of community, how did God respond to the attack? (See Exodus 17:8 – 16; Deuteronomy 25:17 – 19; 1 Samuel 15:1 – 3.)

The text does not say that the attacked Israelites cried out with a *ze'akah*, but what in these passages indicates that God heard such a cry from his people?

Which aspects of the Amalekites' attack do you think were so offensive to God?

What promise did God make regarding the Amalekites, and what does it reveal about the depth of his anger against them?

3. When Moses gave God's decrees and laws to Israel, he mentioned that the Amalekites "had no fear of God" (Deuteronomy 25:18). What do you think it means to have "no fear of God"?

Does it seem to you that God expects people — even those who do not follow him — to have some fear of him? Why or why not?

What does a lack of the "fear of God" allow or promote?

4. Even after the Israelites settled in Canaan, what was their relationship with the Amalekites? (See Judges 3:12 - 14; 6:1 - 6, 33; 7:12.)

Which other peoples and nations allied themselves with the Amalekites, and why? (See Psalm 83.)

What was the true nature of the conflict between these nations and Israel? (See Genesis 3:14 - 15; Psalm 83:1 - 4, 18.)

FOR GREATER UNDERSTANDING
The Impact of the "Fear of God"

When people have an awareness of a "higher power," whether they are committed to the God of the Bible or simply are aware of his existence and moral demands, they have a compelling incentive to do right. The fear of the Lord is a powerful restraint on evil behavior even when self-interest might otherwise provide motivation to exploit the weak. The Torah lists various behaviors that the fear of God should prevent . . . such as causing the blind to stumble, taking advantage of others, charging interest or making a profit off the poor, and enslaving the poor (Leviticus 19:14; 25:17, 35–36, 39, 42–43).

Even in the absence of legal penalties and a foundation for moral standards that govern behavior, the fear of God can motivate people to act in moral, ethical, humane, and caring ways. The midwives in ancient Egypt, for example, who placed their lives at risk in order to spare the newborn Hebrew boys "feared God" (Exodus 1:17). And because they feared the Lord, King Saul's guards refused to obey his command to kill the priests of the Lord (1 Samuel 22:17). When such fear of God is lacking, however, the consequences are great (Psalm 36:1–4; 55:16–19). Abraham felt afraid for himself and Sarah because they were among people who had "no fear of God" (Genesis 20:11).

Reflection

God judged the Amalekites harshly, not only because of their attack on weakened, thirsty Hebrews near Rephidim but because these desert raiders did not "fear" him and, therefore, did not treat innocent people humanely. Their story reveals much about the heart of God and challenges us to "fear the Lord" and live in obedience to his principles, which includes caring for the weak and needy among us.

> What have you learned about God's heart from your study of the Amalekites' attack?

About how deeply he cares for the needs of hurting and weak people in his world?

About how passionately he desires to destroy chaos and restore shalom to his broken world?

Do you think God is any less angry when people attack the weak and cause suffering today than he was during biblical times? Why or why not?

To what extent does the "fear of God" influence your behavior toward the weak, poor, and helpless in your culture?

Who are they, and how do you respond to their needs?

On a scale of one (low) to ten, how highly does your culture "fear God"?

In what ways does the "fear of God" influence your culture's attitudes and actions toward the helpless, unborn, old, poor, AIDS sufferer, disabled, crime victim, or anyone who is perceived of as "lagging behind" in some way?

Memorize

Come, my children, listen to me;
I will teach you the fear of the LORD.
Whoever of you loves life
and desires to see many good days,
keep your tongue from evil
and your lips from speaking lies.
Turn from evil and do good;
seek peace and pursue it.
The eyes of the LORD are on the righteous
and his ears are attentive to their cry;
the face of the LORD is against those who do evil,
to cut off the memory of them from the earth.

Psalm 34:11 – 16

Day Two | Back to Egypt?

The Very Words of God

Therefore, say to the Israelites: "I am the LORD, and I will bring you out
from under the yoke of the Egyptians. I will free you from being slaves
to them, and I will redeem you with an outstretched arm and with
mighty acts of judgment. I will take you as my own people, and I will
be your God. Then you will know that I am the LORD your God who
brought you out from under the yoke of the Egyptians."

Exodus 6:6 – 7

Bible Discovery

The Amalekites: A Vivid Reminder of Egypt's Oppression

After four hundred years in Egypt, the enslaved Hebrews walked
out of Egypt as a free people who were headed to their promised
homeland. When they left the well-watered, fertile fields of Goshen,
they had little idea of how long and difficult their journey through
the desert would be. They had no idea how much they would long
for the "good" life they had experienced in Egypt. They never could
have imagined wanting to be under the yoke of the Egyptians again.

1. When the Israelites faced difficulties in the desert, what did they begin thinking about, and how did they voice their complaints? (See Exodus 14:11; 16:3; 17:3 – 4.)

    As time went on and their difficulties increased, how much stronger was their longing and how much more impassioned were their complaints?

    Although Egypt had plenty of food and water, what would the Israelites have experienced if they had returned there? Do you think that is what they really wanted?

2. We don't know many details regarding the Amalekites' attack on the Israelites in the desert, such as exactly who was in the group that lagged behind and whether the Amalekites killed or captured them (Exodus 17:8; Deuteronomy 25:17 – 18). However, Jewish tradition and a later attack by the Amalekites strongly suggest their motive. (See 1 Samuel 30:1 – 2.)

    a. When the Amalekites raided Ziklag, the home city of David and his men, what did they do to it and its inhabitants?

    b. How did David and his men learn what had happened to their families, and what did this information suggest about the intent of the attack?

c. What did the results of the battle between the Amale-
    kites and David and his men reveal about these cruel des-
    ert raiders?

d. How had the Amalekites treated the women and children
    from Ziklag, and how does this support the view that
    they were taking the wives and children of David and his
    men to Egypt's notorious slave markets?

3. God had said repeatedly that he was bringing his people
    "out of Egypt, out of the land of slavery" (Exodus 13:14; 20:2;
    Deuteronomy 5:6; 6:12, just to list a few).

    a. What point might God have been making concerning
        the Israelites' complaint and longing for Egypt when the
        Amalekites attacked them, and what kind of an impres-
        sion do you think this made on them? (See Deuteronomy
        25:17 – 18.)

    b. How did God intervene in the situation to protect and
        preserve his people, and why was it clear that God acted
        to deliver them (again, in a sense, from the land of slav-
        ery)? (See Exodus 17:9 – 13.)

c.   What would have happened to God's plan of redemption
if the Amalekite raiders had succeeded in taking the Israelites back to Egypt as slaves?

Reflection

You likely have heard the phrase, "Be careful what you wish for
because it might come true." As God was forming the Israelites into
his community of people, they experienced this firsthand at Rephidim. They longed for the water of Egypt and already seemed willing
to forget the price of bondage and brutality they would pay for it.
Then shortly afterward, at the time God was providing a river of
water for his people in the desert, the Amalekites attacked and most
likely would have returned many of them to Egypt as slaves!

From what kinds of "slavery" and suffering has God delivered
you?

When have you been drawn to the desirable things of your past
"bondage in Egypt" rather than wholeheartedly trusting God to
provide for your future needs?

When has God allowed the consequences of your obstinate
refusal to trust him to bear fruit and become a painful lesson of
discipline in your life?

What did you learn about God and your walk with him as a result of that difficult time?

Day Three | Learning to Be a Community

The Very Words of God

> *This is what the LORD Almighty says: "Administer true justice; show mercy and compassion to one another."*

Zechariah 7:9

Bible Discovery

Becoming a Community that Cares in the Way God Cares

Our definitions and vision for community vary widely. To some, a community is little more than the collection of people who live, work, or play in the same general space, such as a neighborhood or group of employees. To others, a community comprises people who are united around a particular objective or cause. These people may have a close connection in relationship to their common interest, but may have little to do with one another in other areas of life. In contrast, God had a much more intimate and involved vision for the people he wanted to shape into the community of his people. The events that took place at Rephidim contribute to our understanding of the community God wanted (and wants) to represent him in the world.

1. We know that some Israelites lagged behind and were attacked by the Amalekites somewhere near Rephidim. It appears that the attack occurred at approximately the same time as the water God provided from Mount Horeb ran to Rephidim. For what reasons do you think the rest of the Israelite community seems to have been unconcerned about

their "weary and worn out" stragglers? (See Exodus 17:1 – 4; Deuteronomy 25:17 – 18.)

2. What remarkable turnabout took place within the entire community after the Amalekite attack, and what did it accomplish? (See Exodus 17:9 – 13.)

Write down the ways, large and small, in which you see God's people working together as a caring community to bring God's justice to bear in the situation with the Amalekites.

In what ways had the Israelites' sense of community and purpose changed since they left Egypt and faced Pharaoh's army by the Red Sea? (See Exodus 13:17 – 18; 14:15 – 28.)

In light of what God wanted to teach the Israelites about being a community that would represent him to the world, how significant is it that the first battle the Israelites fought was in response to the unjust suffering of those who were weak and weary?

3. What is the first thing God commanded to be written in the Hebrew text, and for what reasons do you think God wanted the Israelites to remember this? (See Exodus 17:10 – 14; Deuteronomy 25:19.)

4. God made it clear that he wanted his community of people to be holy because he is holy (Leviticus 19:1). And he would hold them accountable. In his "Song of the Vineyard," the prophet Isaiah portrays the Lord looking for justice and righteousness among his people. What did God *not find*, and what did he *hear*? (See Isaiah 3:14 – 15; 5:1 – 7.)

What happens when the community of God's people — during ancient times as well as today — produces "bad fruit"?

How does God respond when his people refuse to be shaped by him?

Note: This passage has a play on words. In the Hebrew, God looked for *zedekah*, which is the word for "righteousness," but instead he found *ze'akah*, the agonized cry of pain from someone who is being brutally oppressed.

5. A disciple of Jesus passionately wants to be like the Rabbi in his or her walk with God (1 John 2:6), and Jesus responded with great compassion to those who were suffering (Matthew 9:27 – 31; 15:21 – 28; Mark 10:46 – 52). What do Jesus' words in Matthew 25:31 – 46 add to our understanding of how he wants his people to respond to those who are poor, weak, and suffering?

Are the attitudes and actions Jesus wants his community of people to demonstrate any different from what God was teaching the community of Israel in the desert? Why or why not?

Reflection

Today the community of God's people — those who have received Jesus Christ as Lord and Savior — are still under God's mandate to respond to the *ze'akah* that God himself listens for and to which he responds. In our world, *ze'akah* can be heard in every nation and from many sources including the unborn, AIDS sufferers who cannot afford medication, the homeless and unemployed, the hungry, elderly people who are virtually abandoned in nursing homes, and those who are orphaned by war, disease, addiction, and genocide.

What is involved in being a faith *community* of people who love (obey) God in a world where the outcry of suffering is so great?

How willing are you and your faith community to hear and respond to the *ze'akah* of the weak, the oppressed, the weary, the victims of injustice, etc.?

What may be hindering you and your faith community from demonstrating Jesus' loving care and compassion to people who need justice, protection, basic necessities, etc.?

In which specific ways could you and your community of faith become more involved in hearing the cry of suffering people and responding to their needs in practical ways?

How do you think not responding to the cries of hurting people affects a faith community?

What might be your role in improving your faith community's response?

Being the community of God is a high — and rigorous — calling! But it is not impossible. What encouragement for being part of an obedient, life-giving community of God's people do you find in the example of the early Christian community? (See Acts 2:42 – 47.)

Memorize

If you have any encouragement from being united with Christ, if any comfort from his love, if any fellowship with the Spirit, if any tenderness and compassion, then make my joy complete by being like-minded, having the same love, being one in spirit and purpose. Do nothing out of selfish ambition or vain conceit, but in humility consider others better than yourselves. Each of you should look not only to your own interests, but also to the interests of others.

Philippians 2:1 – 4

THINK ABOUT IT

In *The Book of Jewish Values,* author Rabbi Joseph Telushkin points out that the English word "orphan" technically refers to a child who has lost both parents. During biblical times, however, the word included children who had lost fathers but whose mothers were still living, because a child without a father was vulnerable to many forms of exploitation.[3]

Today, at least in most Western countries, there are fewer orphans than in ancient biblical lands. But a staggering number of children are relatively "fatherless" or "motherless" due to broken relationships. Children who are reared by only one parent need all of the support they can get as they develop, in order to handle the significant social and behavioral challenges they face. Does God hear the *ze'akah* of a child who has been robbed of the full provision of two parents? If so, what role do those who seek to be God's partners in restoring shalom to a world broken by chaos have to fulfill in the lives of these hurting children?

Day Four | The Lord Is My Banner

The Very Words of God

Moses built an altar and called it The LORD is my Banner.

Exodus 17:15

Bible Discovery

Keep Your Eyes on God's Banner

During the time of the exodus, the Egyptians used large banners as symbols of their gods' presence. Banners were used to lead the divisions of Egypt's army in battle. They were also placed on enormous poles — some as high as two hundred feet — at the entrance pylons of the temples of Egypt's gods. The banners identified the gods and reminded the Egyptians to keep their eyes on them.

NOTICE THE NICHES ON BOTH SIDES OF THIS GATE PYLON OF THE TEMPLE OF RAMSES AT MEDINET HABU. THESE NICHES HELD THE POLES FOR THE BANNERS OF THE GODS. SOMETIMES THE POLES WERE TWO HUNDRED FEET HIGH, WHICH ENABLED THE COLORFUL BANNERS, DECORATED WITH CARTOUCHES OR SYMBOLS OF THE GODS, TO BE SEEN FROM GREAT DISTANCES. THEIR PURPOSE WAS TO IDENTIFY THE GOD(S) BEING WORSHIPED AND TO POINT WORSHIPERS TO THEIR PRESENCE WITHIN THE TEMPLE. JUST IMAGINE HOW IMPRESSIVE A SIGHT THIS TEMPLE ENTRANCE WOULD BE WITH ITS COLORED HIERO-GLYPHICS AND TALL BANNERS WAVING IN THE WIND.

Moses and the Israelites, of course, would have seen such banners when they lived in Egypt. So when Moses built an altar after the miraculous victory over the Amalekites and called it, "The Lord is my Banner," he was making a powerful statement about the nature of that battle. He was building a reminder that would direct the Israelites' attention toward God.

1. In the ancient Near East, physical symbols were an important way to represent and communicate what otherwise could be somewhat abstract ideas and concepts. Pharaoh's crook and flail, for example, represented his power, authority, and deity. And the banner was such a strong symbol for the presence of a god that it became the hieroglyphic for "god." Similarly, Moses' staff became a central symbol in the exodus story. What did it come to represent and why? (See Exodus 3:1 – 6; 4:1 – 5, 10 – 17; 5:1 – 5; 7:8 – 13, 19 – 20; 8:5 – 6, 17; 9:23; 10:13; 14:16, 21, 26 – 27; 17:5 – 6.)

FOR GREATER UNDERSTANDING
Pharaoh's Crook and Flail vs. Moses' Staff

Moses' staff— "the staff of God" —symbolized God's presence and power. When God told Moses to "throw it on the ground" and the staff became a snake (Exodus 4:3), Moses would have understood that God's power alone made it change into a snake. When Moses used his staff in Pharaoh's presence, Pharaoh certainly would have understood the confrontation of power and authority that was taking place between the gods of Egypt and the Lord.

The crook and flail represented Pharaoh's scepter and symbolized his power, royal authority, and deity. The crook and flail were typically shown held across the chest of Pharaoh or the Egyptian god Osiris.

The flail was made from two or more sticks attached to one another by rope or chain. One stick was held while the others were swung against an object.

continued on next page . . .

The flail was used to thresh grain, as a weapon, and to harm captives and slaves. It illustrated Pharaoh's role as a supposed god who caused the Nile to flood, which in turn produced the crops.

THESE STATUES OF RAMSES HOLDING THE CROOK AND FLAIL ACROSS HIS CHEST ARE TYPICAL OF THE PORTRAYALS OF PHARAOH AND OSIRIS.

The shepherd's crook symbolized power and authority and in hieroglyphics represented "rule." Scholars believe this symbol of deity dates back to when ancient Egypt was a herding culture. Reduced to the size of a scepter, the crook appears in statuary of the monarchy and many of the gods, especially Osiris. As a shepherd rules the flock and must provide for them, so Pharaoh had absolute authority over his people and maintained order — *ma'at* — in the universe for their benefit.

Moses, a shepherd, carried his staff, which became the representation or instrument of God's power in confronting Pharaoh. Pharaoh, on the other hand, used a shepherd's crook to symbolize his authority as a god and king.

2. Before the Amalekites attacked, the Israelites had questioned whether or not God was with them (Exodus 17:7). On the day Israel fought the Amalekites, what did Moses do, and

what message did this action send to God's people? (See Exodus 17:9 – 13.)

Why would it have been significant to the Israelites that Moses' hands (apparently holding the "staff of God") needed to keep pointing like a banner toward the Lord in order for them to win the battle? (See Exodus 17:11 – 12.)

Joshua defeated the Amalekites in that battle, but who was really at war against the Amalekites and gave Israel the victory? (See Exodus 17:13 – 16.)

FOR GREATER UNDERSTANDING

Why Did Moses Raise His Hands?

Scholars have offered several suggestions as to why Moses raised his hands during Israel's battle against the Amalekites (Exodus 17:9 – 12, 15 – 16):

- Raised hands is a Jewish posture of prayer, so Moses was praying for God's help.
- The raised staff had been the instrument of God's power during past situations, such as the Nile turning to blood and the dividing of the Red Sea, so Moses' raised hands with the staff symbolized God's presence and power.
- The raised staff functioned like a military standard or banner. Moses pointed upward to remind the Hebrews that they must keep their eyes on the Lord — who provided the strength for victory — in order to have victory. To see Moses' hands with the staff pointing upward was to see the hand of God at work among them.

3. What partnership between God and the Israelites is evident
    in Exodus 17:14 and Deuteronomy 25:19?

    Why do you think God was willing to partner with the very
    people who were still deep in the chaos of sin in order to
    bring shalom to chaos?

4. What role do you think the Israelites' doubt of God's pres-
    ence with them played in Moses building and naming the
    altar following the battle against the Amalekites? (See Exo-
    dus 17:15.)

    How might this support the idea that Moses, with raised
    hands and "the staff of God," was like a banner pointing to
    the Lord?

DID YOU KNOW?
God's Banner Still Stands

The Hebrew word translated "banner," *nes*, refers to the banner on the pole
and to the pole itself. The pole and bronze snake prominent in Numbers
21:4–9 is *nes*, or "banner pole," which indicates its function as well as
its purpose. So when the Israelites who had been bitten by the venomous
snakes looked at the bronze snake on the pole, they were actually looking at

the *nes*—banner—that pointed upward toward God, whose power healed them.

The prophet Isaiah wrote of another banner that was yet to come (Isaiah 11:1–5, 10, 12). This banner would rise up from the root of Jesse, and his mission would be to point to the presence of God and direct the eyes of the nations toward him. In John 3:14–16, Jesus used the metaphor of the banner pole—the one mentioned in Isaiah 11—to say that he would be lifted up on a pole (cross) like the snake. This claim revealed that Jesus, the Son of God, was indeed the Messiah, the Savior of all who believe. He is the banner (*nes*) who points to the Father and signifies his Father's presence.

GOD GAVE THE TRIBE OF JUDAH THE TASK OF LEADING THE PEOPLE AS THEY TRAVELED IN THE DESERT. JUDAH, THE TRIBE FROM WHICH THE MESSIAH WOULD COME, WHILE NOT WITHOUT SIN, WAS MORE OBEDIENT THAN MANY OF THE OTHER TRIBES THROUGHOUT THE HISTORY OF ISRAEL. THE ARTIST CREATED THIS BANNER WITH A LION, THE SYMBOL THE BIBLE ASSIGNS TO THE TRIBE OF JUDAH (AND, BY EXTENSION, TO THE MESSIAH HIMSELF; SEE GENESIS 49:9; REVELATION 5:5). ISAIAH INDICATES THAT THE COMING MESSIAH WILL BE A BANNER—SOMEONE TO LOOK TO AND IDENTIFY WITH—TO THE NATIONS (ISAIAH 11:10–12).

Reflection

Moses, and no doubt the rest of the Israelites, recognized God's awesome power as he gave them victory over the Amalekites. The Israelites had taken a huge step in their relationship with God: they had come together as a community to partner with God in accomplishing his purpose. Instead of watching from the sidelines as God worked miraculously on their behalf (as in the plagues and the defeat of Pharaoh's army at the Red Sea), they were active participants, fighting and achieving victory by the power of God. Imagine how they felt as they saw Moses' hands and staff pointing toward "the throne of the Lord" and knew that God was with them!

To what extent do you think God still partners with his people in order to accomplish his purposes? What examples can you think of?

Who actually accomplishes God's purposes and provides the victory when God partners with his people, and what other biblical examples come to mind?

How important is it for God's people to step up and support another person in his/her work for the Lord, just as Aaron and Hur did for Moses?

What might be your role in doing this?

To what extent have you questioned whether or not God was with you when you have faced a difficult challenge in your walk with him?

How did God reveal his presence and power to you at the time?

What symbol represented God's power, care, and involvement in your life at that time?

In what ways can that symbol serve as a "banner" for you, helping to keep your eyes focused on God and your heart trusting in his presence and power for the strength to carry on?

Day Five | God's Judgment on the Amalekites

The Very Words of God

The Lord will be at war against the Amalekites from generation to generation.

Exodus 17:16

Bible Discovery

God Fulfills His Promise through His People

When they attacked the Israelites on their way to Rephidim, the Amalekites not only hurt the weak and defenseless, they directly attacked God and his redemptive work. God's plan to restore shalom to his world required the Messiah — the Savior — to come through his chosen people, Israel, whom the Amalekites sought to wipe out. So consider God's actions against the Amalekites, including the tribes of Israel that played key roles in those confrontations.

1. God did not intend for any of his people to be abandoned in the desert and left vulnerable to attack. Whether they faced enemies in front or in the rear, God had established guidance and protection for his people. Which tribe was to bring up the rear and protect God's people,[4] and which tribe was to lead? (See Numbers 2:9; 10:14, 25.)

   Which symbols had been given earlier to Jacob's sons Judah and Dan, and in what ways did each tribe seem to live up to these symbols? (See Genesis 49:1, 8 – 10, 17; Revelation 5:5.)

PROFILE OF A PEOPLE

Insight into the Tribe of Dan

According to Judges 18, the tribe of Dan was to inherit Zorah and Eshtaol in the shephelah, the foothills between the coastal plain where the Philistines lived and the mountains of Judah where the tribe of Judah lived. In a sense, Dan was to be on the frontlines, bringing God's kingdom to the pagans who lived west of them. But the Danites were not pleased with their inheritance and apparently were not up to or interested in the task God had assigned to them. They wanted an easier task and looked for a land more to their liking.

The Danites found what they wanted in the northern part of the Promised Land. They brutally conquered Laish, the main city in the region, and renamed it Dan. At the time, they probably did not realize that the main route from the north and east into Israel passed right through this area. So they once again were on Israel's frontlines. All of Israel's future enemies—Assyrians, Babylonians, Persians, Greeks, and Romans—came to Dan first.

The tribe of Dan was commissioned to bring up the rear of the community of Israel as they traveled in the desert but, as was consistently the case, Dan did not live up to God's desire. The tribe failed to protect the people from the Amalekites. The tribe of Dan is identified by their banner on a pole. The artist portrayed the banner with a serpent to identify the tribe, because that was the symbol Jacob used to describe them (Genesis 49:17). Tradition notes that the serpent symbol summarizes Dan's refusal to submit to God. The tribe is left off the tribal list in John's vision of heaven (Revelation 7).

2. After the Israelites settled in the Promised Land, God kept
    his promise regarding the Amalekites. What did he, through
    the prophet Samuel, command King Saul (a Benjamite) to do
    concerning Amalek? (See 1 Samuel 15:1 - 5.)

    What did Saul do instead, and what seems to be his motiva-
    tion? (On what banner were his eyes focused?) (See 1 Sam-
    uel 15:7 - 9, 13 - 23.)

    How did God respond to Saul, and what does this convey
    regarding the seriousness of God's command to remem-
    ber — *zakar* — by obedient action? (See 1 Samuel 15:10 - 11,
    22 - 29.)

DID YOU KNOW?
The Action of Remembering

When God commanded Moses to write down that the Israelites were to
"remember what the Amalekites did to you" (Deuteronomy 25:17), he was
not just emphasizing intellectual activity or recalling in one's mind. The
Hebrew word translated "remember," *zakar*, implies recalling and taking
action on that basis. To *zakar* means to become personally involved because
of what one is remembering.[5] It also suggests learning by being involved
in what is remembered. The word is often followed by a command to take
action. For examples of the obligations implied by remembering, read: Exodus 13:3; 20:8; Numbers 15:39–40; Deuteronomy 5:15; 8:11–18; 16:12;
24:17–19; Nehemiah 1:7–9; 4:14; Psalm 22:27; 103:17–18; 119:55; Matthew 5:22–24; Luke 22:18–20; Revelation 2:5.

3. Nearly five hundred years after the attack at Rephidim, God fulfilled his promise to Israel regarding the Amalekites. The story is recorded in the book of Esther.

   a. What did Haman (a descendant of Agag the Amalekite) plot? (See Esther 3:1 – 15.)

   b. How did Mordecai and the rest of the Jews respond? (See Esther 4:1 – 3.)

   c. Would this outcry have been a compelling *ze'akah* to the ears of God? For what reasons?

   d. What victory did God accomplish through Queen Esther (a Benjamite, like Saul)? (See Esther 7:3 – 10; 8:7 – 17.)

   e. In what ways did the community of Jews come together to participate in the amazing work God was accomplishing in their midst? (See Esther 4:4 – 17; 9:1 – 16.)

4.   When facing Haman and their other enemies, how did
     Queen Esther and other Jews demonstrate obedience to God
     because they "remembered" what the Amalekites had done,
     as God had commanded? (Compare Exodus 17:8 – 9 with
     Esther 5:7 – 8; 1 Samuel 15:3 with Esther 9:5 – 10, 14 – 15.)

Reflection

God fulfills all of his promises — even if it takes five hundred years!
He remains faithful, and he commands us to be faithful to him. He
delights in using human partners to accomplish his purposes, just
as he used the Israelites in fulfilling his judgment against the Amalekites.

As you read the story about the final defeat of the Amalekites, did
your mind go back to what happened in the desert near Rephidim?
If not, take a moment to review what happened that day.

> Was the final conclusion to that battle near Rephidim any more
> or less amazing than what happened when God fulfilled his
> promise during Esther's time? Why?

> What impact does the whole story — beginning to end — have
> on your knowledge (experience) with God?

> When it came to dealing with the Amalekites, some of God's
> people failed along the way. Their disobedience, even though it
> was forgiven, had serious repercussions for God's people at the

time and into the future. What were some of those repercussions, and how do they help you to realize the potential long-term consequences of your sin?

Why is your faithfulness to God so important to him?

In what ways do you struggle to be faithful "where" God wants you to be?

In what ways do you struggle to be faithful in taking the actions God wants you to take?

Memorize

Remember what the Amalekites did to you along the way when you came out of Egypt.... When the LORD your God gives you rest from all the enemies around you in the land he is giving you to possess as an inheritance, you shall blot out the memory of Amalek from under heaven. Do not forget!

Deuteronomy 25:17 – 19

THE MOUNTAIN OF GOD
Exodus 19–20

God had heard the *ze'akah* cry of his Hebrew people who suffered under brutal Egyptian slave masters. Although Pharaoh persisted in his refusal to let the Hebrews go into the desert to meet with their God, he and the gods of Egypt were impotent to stop even the "finger" of God at work. So through miraculous demonstrations of his great power, God brought his people out of Egypt, across the Red Sea, and into the deserts of Sinai.

The Hebrews knew about the desert, but they were not desert people. For centuries they had been farmers, herdsmen, and craftsmen who lived in some of the finest, most productive land in the world. How would they survive in the desert? It wouldn't be easy, but God, the Shepherd of Israel, knew his "flock" well. In the symbol of a pillar of cloud by day and fire by night, he assured them of his presence and led them every step of the way. He planned experiences in the desert to humble them, test them, and train them in how to obey his commands and live as *his* people so that the world would come to know their God.

How would the Israelites respond to God's calling and his training? Would they accept his reign as their Lord and King? After the miraculous Red Sea crossing, they joyfully proclaimed their reigning God as *Lord* (Exodus 15). Then they followed the cloud into the desert where God continued to shape and prepare them to become his partners in not only *bringing* the message of his kingdom to the world but in *being* his message. After forty days of testing and training in how to live according to his every word, it was time for the Israelites to get to know their God as they never had before: it was time for them to go up to the mountain of God!

Moses had been to the mountain of God, or Mount Sinai, before. That was where he saw fire in the bush and first spoke with God, and where God had said Moses would bring Israel to meet him. No physical phenomena can fully communicate the awe-inspiring character of the Creator of the universe, but the mountain shook, cloud and smoke covered it, and out of the glory of fire at its top the voice of God spoke. The awestruck Israelites knew without a doubt that he was the God of their ancestors, the Creator who had redeemed them from Egypt.

The importance of God's revelation to the Israelites on Mount Sinai can scarcely be overestimated. Both the Hebrew and Christian texts refer to it frequently. It is the basis on which God's prophets demanded obedience, challenged disobedience, and reminded Israel of his great love and passion for them. It became the foundation of Judeo-Christian culture and for nearly two millennia shaped much of Western civilization. It is one of the most important events in world history.

God's revelation on Mount Sinai also taught the Hebrews that he cared about how they — and we — live our lives. Then, as now, God was training his people to bring his shalom to this sinful, broken world. So it should not surprise us that in Moses' last will and testament, which is essentially what Deuteronomy is, he warned God's people not to forget that God spoke to them at Mount Sinai. Moses told them to teach God's revelation — not only what they heard God say, but that he spoke out of the fire on the mountain — to their children and grandchildren.

By his grace, God delivered the Hebrews from bondage in Egypt and began to form them into his people. Likewise, Jesus delivered those of us who follow him from our bondage to sin and is shaping us into his people. God desires that we, like Israel, *bring* and *be* his message. But we must not forget the "fire." Our God is mighty in power, magnificent in holiness, and passionate in his love for his people. Israel met this God in the fire on Mount Sinai; the early Christian community met this God in the tongues of fire on the mountain of

God in Jerusalem at Pentecost. The fire of God still blazes, and God still desires to meet us so that the passion of our hearts is ignited to pass on all that our awesome God has done.

Opening Thoughts (3 minutes)

The Very Words of God

> *Only be careful, and watch yourselves closely so that you do not forget the things your eyes have seen or let them slip from your heart as long as you live. Teach them to your children and to their children after them. Remember the day you stood before the LORD your God at Horeb, when he said to me, "Assemble the people before me to hear my words so that they may learn to revere me as long as they live in the land and may teach them to their children." You came near and stood at the foot of the mountain while it blazed with fire to the very heavens, with black clouds and deep darkness. Then the LORD spoke to you out of the fire.*

Deuteronomy 4:9 – 12

Think About It

When we have something very important to say to someone we care about, we often choose carefully the time and place to say it. We want the person's undivided attention, we want an environment that will enhance rather than detract from our message, and we want to express ourselves in a way that will not be forgotten.

If God were to choose a time and place to say something important to you, how do you think he might do it? How might he get your undivided attention? What kind of setting might help you to hear his voice? What might help you to remember his words forever?

DVD Notes (28 minutes)

Up to the mountain of God

Moses meets God on Mount Sinai

Fire of God on the mountain

Story shaping story: Mount Sinai as a paradigm for Jesus

Three "legs" of God's kingdom

DVD Discussion (6 minutes)

1. By the time the Israelites reached Mount Sinai, they had
    been in the desert for about forty days. On the map of Lower
    Egypt and the Sinai Peninsula, locate Jebel Katarina and
    Jebel Musa in the mountains of southern Sinai. Remember,
    although these are not necessarily the actual mountains
    where Moses and the Israelites met God, they reveal what
    those mountains would have been like.

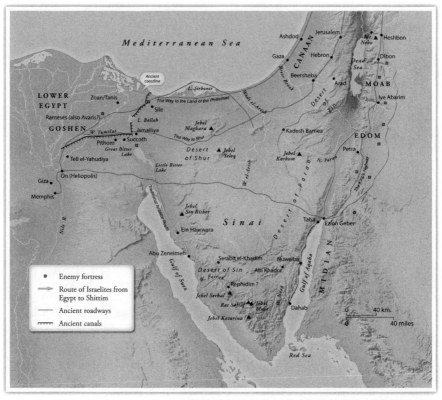

LOWER EGYPT AND THE SINAI PENINSULA

Think what it would have been like to have spent weeks in
the Sinai desert, and then to have arrived at the mountain
of God — the mountain where God speaks to his people. If
you had been there, what effect would a shaking mountain

enveloped in clouds of darkness that blazed with fire and roared with thunder have had on you?

If you had heard the voice of God speak to you as you stood before *that* mountain in *that* desert, what would you have thought? What would you have remembered?

2. As you recall the video of the long climb up Jebel Katarina, imagine Moses climbing Mount Sinai at least four times at eighty years of age! What insight does this give you into Moses' relationship with God and his commitment to obey God's every word?

3. What messages did God deliver to Moses and the Israelites at Mount Sinai, and how important were they? (List as many as you recall!)

What was God seeking to accomplish through the instructions he gave at Mount Sinai?

HINT: Think about the three legs of God's kingdom: the finger of God acting with awesome power in the plagues and the crossing of the Red Sea; God's people responding to these acts by calling him "Lord"; God, through his people, building his kingdom on earth.

4. In what way(s) do you see the events at Mount Sinai as being a paradigm for, or shaping, events in the life of Jesus the Messiah?

FOR GREATER UNDERSTANDING
Survival in the Deserts of Sinai

It is difficult for someone who has not walked in the deserts of the Sinai to imagine how hostile and difficult this wilderness is. Moses described it as vast, dreadful, thirsty, and waterless, with venomous snakes and scorpions (Deuteronomy 8:15). That is a good description. Daily temperatures can range from 50 degrees Fahrenheit at midnight to 125 degrees Fahrenheit at noon. Frequent strong winds and almost no shade exaggerate the effect of the cold and heat. Because almost nothing grows there, it is nearly

continued on next page . . .

impossible to find wood to build a warming fire at night. The terrain is rarely flat for any distance, and one must cross steep, rocky ridges in order to travel from one place to another.

THE "VAST AND DREADFUL DESERT, THAT THIRSTY AND WATERLESS LAND."

It's easy for us to read about Israel's time in the desert and find fault with their complaints and failures, but to walk where they walked for any length of time is to gain admiration for their stamina and perseverance. Few of us would be willing to spend long periods of time in such difficult circumstances just because God commanded it. We benefit from the pain and sacrifice they suffered in learning to obey and trust their God. Without his provision of manna and water from the rock, they could not have survived. No wonder he told them, "I carried you on eagles' wings and brought you to myself" (Exodus 19:4).

Small Group Bible Discovery and Discussion (17 minutes)

Getting to Know Mount Sinai

Few locations have played such a significant role in human history as Mount Sinai — the mountain of God. Events that happened there, and the ways in which Moses and God's people experienced God there, continue to reverberate throughout the world.

1. There are at least three names for the mountain where God
   met with Moses and the Israelites. As you consider just a few
   of these encounters, take note of what was known about the
   mountain and its physical characteristics, the name used for
   the mountain, and what took place between God and his
   people there.

The Text	The Mountain's Location/Physical Characteristics	Name for This Mountain	What Took Place between God and His People Here
Ex. 3:1–10*			
Ex. 4:27–31*			
Ex. 17:5–6*			
Ex. 18:5–12			
Ex. 19:10–12, 16–19*			
Ex. 24:15–18*			
Ex. 34:1–6			
1 Kings 19:3–4, 7–16			

*NOTE: If your group time is very limited, include only these portions
of Scripture in your study.

2. As a result of reading these passages, what new things did you realize about the mountain of God?

What possible connection do you see between what the mountain is called in a given instance and what happened there at that time?

How widely known does the mountain appear to be to people who lived in that region during ancient times?

DID YOU KNOW?
Sacred Mountains in Ancient Cultures

Many ancient cultures shared the myth of a sacred mountain on which the gods lived—where heaven met earth. Whether it was Mount Olympus in Greece, Mount Saphon in the Ugaritic civilization, or Mount Hermon (meaning "sacred mountain" in Hebrew) in northern Israel, people seem to have shared a common understanding that their gods were exalted above the earth and that on high mountains people might come closer to their deities or their deities might choose to "come down" to meet with them. The theme also occurs in Egyptian mythology concerning the origin of the cosmos. Because the gods were believed to have drawn the universe out of chaos from a sacred mound or hill, Egyptian temples were designed so that worshipers moved up to the holy sanctuary—the highest point of the temple. The idea of humanity striving to be closer to their deities also may be the perspective behind the biblical story of the tower of Babel (Genesis 11). So God's choice to meet his people at a high mountain was completely logical in light of the worldviews with which the Israelites were familiar.

Faith Lesson (5 minutes)

Since the days when he met with Moses and the ancient Israelites on Mount Sinai, God has not changed. His passionate love for humanity, commitment to test and train his people, and faithfulness in restoring shalom to his world is just as strong today as it was during ancient times. His might and power to act on behalf of his people to fulfill his plan of redemption has not diminished.

Many of us, however, seem to be unaware of God's awesome holiness and power, oblivious to our own unworthiness to be in his presence. We have not "met with God" on his mountain. Perhaps we can come to know God and renew our passion and commitment to obey his every word by seeking as much as possible to experience what the Israelites experienced when they went to the mountain to meet with God.

Exodus 20:18–21 gives us a good start in understanding what it was like to meet with God on his mountain:

> *When the people saw the thunder and lightning and heard the trumpet and saw the mountain in smoke, they trembled with fear. They stayed at a distance and said to Moses, "Speak to us yourself and we will listen. But do not have God speak to us or we will die." Moses said to the people, "Do not be afraid. God has come to test you, so that the fear of God will be with you to keep you from sinning." The people remained at a distance, while Moses approached the thick darkness where God was.*

1. What intense sensory phenomena — hearing, seeing, feeling — occurred as Moses and Israel met with God at the mountain?

    What do you think it would have been like to stand before the mountain and know that all of that activity was because of God's presence there?

What does it cause you to realize about the nature of God?

What does it cause you to realize about yourself?

2. What was the difference between the people's response to God at the mountain and Moses' response?

What do you think accounts for their different responses?

What do these differences help you to understand about your relationship with God?

3. Based on this scene at Mount Sinai, how important is it to God that his people be holy as he is holy?

How much effort is God willing to expend to teach his people to obey him?

How does his effort help you to realize the level of effort and commitment to obedience he may require of you?

4. What would God's choosing to meet the Israelites at Mount
    Sinai have symbolized to them, and how would it have fit
    their cultural expectations?

In what culturally relevant ways does God "come down to
the mountain" to meet his people today?

What impact does his presence and message make on you?

Closing (1 minute)

Read Exodus 19:18 – 19 together aloud: "Mount Sinai was covered
with smoke, because the LORD descended on it in fire. The smoke
billowed up from it like smoke from a furnace, the whole mountain
trembled violently, and the sound of the trumpet grew louder and
louder. Then Moses spoke and the voice of God answered him."

Then pray together, asking God to help you know (experience) what
it was like for the Israelites to meet with him at Mount Sinai. Ask
him to help you become more aware of his presence, his holiness,
and his call to complete obedience.

Memorize

> *Mount Sinai was covered with smoke, because the LORD descended on
> it in fire. The smoke billowed up from it like smoke from a furnace, the
> whole mountain trembled violently, and the sound of the trumpet grew
> louder and louder. Then Moses spoke and the voice of God answered
> him.*
>
> *Exodus 19:18 – 19*

DID YOU KNOW?
Representations of the Sacred Mountain in Egyptian Temples

According to Egyptian creation myth, their god Atum stood on a sacred hill to bring the cosmos into existence, and this is reflected in the very structure of Egypt's temples. The passage from the temple entrance through the courts and into the inner sanctuary rises to its highest point in the most sacred chamber where the presence of the god was believed to reside. The gradual rise portrayed concretely to worshipers the sacred mound from which the god originally created the universe.

THE FUNERARY TEMPLE OF THE FAMOUS FEMALE PHARAOH, HATSHEPSUT, IS LOCATED NEAR THE VALLEY OF THE KINGS AND THE VALLEY OF THE QUEENS. MANY PHARAOHS AND THEIR QUEENS WERE BURIED IN THIS AREA AT THE FOOT OF A PYRAMID-SHAPED MOUNTAIN, WHICH RETAINED THE SYMBOLISM OF THE PYRAMIDS WHERE EARLIER PHARAOHS WERE INTERRED. NOTICE THE STEPS LEADING WORSHIPERS UP TO THE SACRED HILL.

The inner sanctuary, which in Egyptian temples was usually small and dark, functioned as a "high place" representing the mythical sacred hill. Inner sanctuaries were accessible only to Pharaoh and the highest echelon of priests. The highest standards of purity were required for all who entered the sanctuary, which the Egyptians thought of as "heaven on earth." Images of the god (often made of gold) marked its presence within the sanctuary.

THE SMALL, DARK, INNER SANCTUARY OF HATSHEPSUT'S FUNERARY TEMPLE. NOTICE THE GRADUAL RISE FROM THE INNER COURT INTO THE MOST HOLY HIGH PLACE.

Tested and Trained to Be God's Message

In-Depth Personal Study Sessions

Day One | Mountains: Where God Comes Down to Meet His People

The Very Words of God

> *After they set out from Rephidim, they entered the Desert of Sinai, and Israel camped there in the desert in front of the mountain. Then Moses went up to God, and the LORD called to him from the mountain.*

> *Exodus 19:2–3*

Bible Discovery

A Meeting Place God's People Understood

Like other people of their time, the Israelites were familiar with the cultural practice of seeking God (or gods) on high places. So they naturally understood that God would call them to mountains and mountaintops so that they could worship him and he could teach them. God related to his people through mountain experiences just as he related to them through other familiar cultural icons and practices, such as temple worship, priests, sacrifices, offerings, altars, and prophets.

1. We can view the places where God chose to meet with his people during biblical times as isolated events, and we can learn valuable lessons from what took place. But, as in everything God does, these events and their locations were not accidental, and we can come to know so much more of our God if we view individual events as pieces of a much bigger story. Consider, for example, Genesis 22:1 – 2, 12 – 14 and 1 Chronicles 21:1, 6 – 22:1; 2 Chronicles 3:1.

a. What happened on this mountain during the time of Abraham?

b. What future significance would this mountain have during the time of the kings of Israel, during the time of Jesus and the disciples, during our times, and in the future?

c. Think of the name Abraham gave to this mountain. In what ways has this mountain been (and will continue to be) the mountain of God's provision?

d. In what new ways have you experienced God through this brief exploration of just one place where God has met his people time and time again? What is your response to this new experience, and what difference will it make in your walk with God?

DATA FILE
The Mountains Where God Meets His People

For the Israelites, the original mountain of God was Mount Sinai, and during the early part of Israel's forty years in the desert that mountain played a central role in God's shaping and molding of his people. Mount Sinai frequently reminded them of their God and his relationship to them and expectations for

continued on next page . . .

them. But as the Israelites moved into the Promised Land, God expanded his revelation and taught them to be his witnesses to the world. Then another mountain—Mount Zion (previously known as Mount Moriah)—became known to his people as the place where God would dwell on earth (Psalm 74:2; Isaiah 8:18; 24:23).

King Solomon, David's son, built the Lord's temple on Mount Zion, on the threshing floor where God had appeared to David. Then God invited the world to "go up" to the mountain into his presence. It is possible that the loss of memory of Mount Sinai's exact location occurred because of the increasing role the Lord's temple on Mount Zion assumed in the lives of his people and in their witness to the world.

In a sense, part of God's great work of creating, redeeming, and shaping his people to be his own begins at Mount Sinai, continues at Mount Zion, and culminates at another "sacred mountain"—heavenly Jerusalem (Hebrews 12:22). For further study on the similarities and differences between Mount Sinai and Mount Zion, consider the following comparisons:

Similarities

Compare Exodus 19:23 to Psalm 48:1, 87:1–2; Exodus 24:15–18 to Psalm 43:3; Exodus 19:17–19, 20:18–19; 24:15–18 to 2 Chronicles 7:1–3 and Isaiah 4:5; Exodus 20; 31:18 to Isaiah 2:1–5; Exodus 3:1, 19:1–2 to Exodus 15:17.

Differences

Compare Exodus 19:10–13, 16–24; 20:18–21; 24:1–2 and Hebrews 12:18–21 to Isaiah 2:2–4, Jeremiah 31:6; and Micah 4:2.

For further study on how the mountain of God points to what God will do in the future, consider: Isaiah 11:1–10; 25:1–9; 65:17–25; Micah 4:1–5; and Zechariah 8:1–23.

2. For each of the following passages, take note of what you discover and what God's purpose might be for each mountain or mountain encounter.

    a. *Ezekiel 28:13 – 15.* What insight does this provide into why it was so significant that Adam and Eve hid from God after they sinned?

    b. *Exodus 3:1 – 12; 19:1 – 6.* What was God's purpose in drawing Moses and the Israelites to this mountain?

    c. *Numbers 20:22 – 29.* Why might God have wanted to "gather" Aaron, high priest of Israel, from a mountaintop?

    d. *Deuteronomy 34:1 – 8.* Why might you want your last day on earth to be a time of communication with God similar to what Moses experienced? In what ways is this final conversation like so many that preceded it, and what effort did Moses put forth to have this kind of relationship with God?

    e. *Joshua 8:30 – 35.* What kind of statement was Joshua making by building the altar and renewing the covenant on a mountain? What do you think it would have meant to the Israelites at the time?

3. Often we see in Scripture the text of one story shaping the text of a later story. So it should not surprise us to see similarities between the way Moses encountered God on the mountain and the way Jesus (the promised prophet like Moses, see Acts 3:22; 7:37) did. As you consider the following comparisons, keep in mind that these individual events occur within the bigger story of God's plan to redeem his world.

   a. In Matthew 5:1 – 12, Jesus went up to teach on the mountain. What did Moses do to receive God's instruction?

   b. What happened to Jesus on the mountain (Matthew 17:1 – 9) that is similar to some of Moses' experiences on Mount Sinai? In what ways was the experience of Jesus' disciples similar to that of the Israelites?

   c. By the time Jesus ascended into heaven (Acts 1:1 – 11), his disciples were certain of who he was. Why might he have gone to heaven from a mountain, and what might be his connection to how Moses and Aaron spent their last days on earth?

Reflection

Since the day he created Adam, God has desired to meet with his people. During ancient times, he often chose to meet them on a mountain. Some of God's people walked many miles through harsh and terrible deserts to climb his mountain and meet with him there. Sustained by God, they considered it worthwhile to exert great effort in following God to his mountain where they could hear his voice and learn to obey his every word.

What about us? What effort does it take to meet God on his mountain today? Hebrews 12:18 – 20 tells us that we have not come to the unbearable sight of "a mountain that can be touched and that is burning with fire," one that was so terrifying even Moses trembled with fear. Instead, we come to God on "Mount Zion, to the heavenly Jerusalem, the city of the living God" (Hebrews 12:22).

Take time to thoroughly and thoughtfully read Hebrews 12:18 – 29. This text introduces us to God on Mount Zion and instructs us in our heritage as his people who desire to come before him but also must learn to worship him "acceptably with reverence and awe." Then think about the following questions and the implications for your relationship with God.

> In comparison to God's meeting with the Israelites at Mount Sinai, what has — and has not — changed for followers of Jesus who come to God's mountain?

> The descriptions of Israel meeting God at his mountain are full of vivid sensory imagery. What does this convey about our God and the nature of our relationship with him that we may miss out on because we typically do not think of God in these terms?

> Which images or physical experiences of God's exalted nature and his desire to meet with his people do we use today, and which are most meaningful to you?

In what ways does Hebrews 12 add to these images and to your knowledge (experience) of God and your relationship with him?

How do you think a person worships God "acceptably with reverence and awe"?

How do you think God teaches his people to do this today?

How much effort are you willing to exert to learn to do this?

What warning does the writer of Hebrews offer, and what does that advice require you to do?

Memorize

But you have come to Mount Zion, to the heavenly Jerusalem, the city of the living God. You have come to thousands upon thousands of angels in joyful assembly, to the church of the firstborn, whose names are written in heaven. You have come to God, the judge of all men, to the spirits of righteous men made perfect, to Jesus the mediator of a new covenant, and to the sprinkled blood that speaks a better word than the blood of Abel.

See to it that you do not refuse him who speaks.... Therefore, since we are receiving a kingdom that cannot be shaken, let us be thankful, and so worship God acceptably with reverence and awe, for our "God is a consuming fire."

Hebrews 12:22 – 25, 28 – 29

DATA FILE

What Do We Know about High Places?

The same logic that led ancient people to designate sacred mountains apparently led them to worship their gods in "high places." Although worship on high places was not always bad (Abraham sacrificed to God on Mount Moriah, for example), nearly all of Scripture's seventy references to high places refer to pagan rituals that did not honor God. Such rituals included immoral practices, standing stones, fertility rites, images, and Asherah poles. So God commanded his people to avoid pagan practices at high places. He did not want pagan gods to lure his people away from worshiping him at his high place in Jerusalem.

Scholars disagree about the exact nature of religious high places, but the biblical text provides enough information to allow us to draw some conclusions.

Characteristics of High Places	Evidence of the Text
Often located on natural hills or mountains	Deut. 12:1–3; 1 Kings 14:22–23; 2 Kings 23:13; 2 Chron. 28:4; Ezek. 6:13
Contained man-made structures	Num. 33:52; Deut. 12:3; 1 Kings 12:31; 2 Kings 21:3; 2 Chron. 14:2–5
Often associated with pagan ritual and practice	1 Kings 12:32; 14:22–24; 2 Kings 14:3–4; Ps. 78:57–58; Jer. 19:5
If high places were pagan, they were to be destroyed; if Israel rebuilt or used them, God would become angry.	Lev. 26:30–33; Deut. 12:1–4; 2 Kings 17:7–13; Ezek. 6:1–7
Israel sometimes used them to worship the Lord.	1 Kings 3:2, 4; 2 Chron. 1:3; 33:17
Leaders who destroyed the pagan high places were considered faithful to God; those who didn't were deemed unfaithful.	1 Kings 15:11–15; 22:42–43; 2 Kings 12:2–4; 14:1–4; 18:1–5; 21:1–3; 23:4–8, 19–25; 2 Chron. 34:1–4

Day Two | The Israelites Come to Mount Sinai

The Very Words of God

> Then Moses went up to God, and the LORD called to him from the
> mountain and said, "This is what you are to say to the house of Jacob
> and what you are to tell the people of Israel: "You yourselves have
> seen what I did to Egypt, and how I carried you on eagles' wings and
> brought you to myself. Now if you obey me fully and keep my covenant,
> then out of all nations you will be my treasured possession. Although
> the whole earth is mine, you will be for me a kingdom of priests and a
> holy nation." These are the words you are to speak to the Israelites.

Exodus 19:3 – 6

Bible Discovery

Israel: God's Treasured Possession

Israel arrived at Mount Sinai, the mountain of God, at the beginning
of the third month, approximately six weeks after the angel of death
"passed over" them and claimed the firstborn of Egypt (Exodus
19:1 - 8). They camped at the foot of Mount Sinai for nearly a year
as God revealed to them the response he expected of them — the
people he chose to be his treasured possession and had graciously
delivered from slavery. Although they had not always been faithful
to God in Egypt, nor had they trusted him completely after leaving
Egypt, God had loved them dearly for a long time! They had celebrated him as their King at the Red Sea, and now they needed to
learn how to accept his reign as their Lord.

1. What did Moses do immediately after reaching Mount Sinai,
    and what revelation did God give him to share with the
    people? (See Exodus 19:1 - 8.)

How did the people respond to what God, through Moses, revealed to them?

Given the Israelites' previous response and commitments to God, is this how you would have expected them to respond? (See Exodus 4:29 – 31; 14:29 – 31; 15.) Why or why not?

To what extent do you think they realized what this commitment would require of them?

DID YOU KNOW?

The Hebrew word *segulah*, which is used to describe Israel as God's "treasured possession" (Exodus 19:5), has a rich meaning. At the personal level, *segulah* referred to someone's prized possession. At the cultural and political level, a king would designate his closest subject kingdom as his *segulah* and thus provide special treatment (including protection and legal rights) to that kingdom and that kingdom alone. So, by describing Israel as *segulah*, God offered his people an incredible promise. He offered them the opportunity to be his chosen partners in restoring his world — if they would accept his reign in their lives.

---

2. According to Exodus 3:7, 10; 5:1; 7:4, did Israel come to Sinai to *become* God's people or were they already God's people before arriving there? Explain your answer.

For what reasons was God committed to caring for the Israelites, and what promises had he made concerning them? (See Genesis 17:1 – 8; Exodus 2:24; 6:2 – 8.)

What amazing metaphor did God use to describe the Israelites in Egypt? (See Exodus 4:22 – 23.)

Which images did God use to describe his care for the Israelites during their journey in the desert, and to what did he compare himself and Israel? (See Exodus 19:4; Deuteronomy 32:7 – 11.)

What did God demonstrate by the way in which he delivered Israel from Egypt? (See Exodus 7:1 – 5.)

What do these descriptions of God's care and commitment on behalf of his people reveal to you about the depth and tenderness of his love for them?

FOR GREATER UNDERSTANDING
The "Wings" of God

Many scholars consider the image of God as a mother eagle to be one of the most compelling in the Hebrew Bible. It is believed that mother eagles train their eaglets to fly by pushing them out of the nest at just the right time to try their wings. At first, because each eaglet flounders, she flies under it, rescues it, and carries it back to safety with her strong wings.

In similar fashion, God nudged the Hebrews out of Egypt. In the "vast and dreadful wilderness," Israel was completely helpless and vulnerable without his care. Yet God took Israel as his own and, like an eagle nurtures an eaglet, he provided refuge in his "wings." Slowly but surely, while safe in the protection of his wings, God taught them to "fly." God asked them to assume increasing responsibility for their obedience while remaining completely dependent on his protection (notice the contrast between Exodus 14:13–14 and 17:8–13). When they faltered because of bitter water, no bread, and no water, he metaphorically swooped down, picked them up, and guided them safely to Sinai.

At Mount Sinai, it was time for the Israelites to receive the revelation of God's will for them and to take up their role as his witnesses in a broken world. Wherever they went, they took the image of God's "wings" with them. In the ark of the covenant, the place God's presence would dwell after Israel left Mount Sinai, the spread wings of the cherubim reminded God's people that his nurturing care had brought them to himself (Exodus 25:10–22).

The protective "wing of God" image shows up in other ways as well. In Hebrew, the word *kanaf* means both "wing" and "corner." So when Ruth asked Boaz to spread the "corner" of his robe over her (Ruth 3:9), she was asking him to bring her under his protection. Malachi predicted that the "sun of righteousness," a figure many identified as the Messiah — would have healing in his "wings" or "corners" (Malachi 4:2). Perhaps this is the image that motivated the woman who was healed by touching the edge or "corner" of Jesus' robe. She recognized his identity as the Messiah and reached out for the protection and healing of his "wings" (Matthew 9:20–22).

3. Israel was God's treasured possession because God was
    faithful to the promises he had made to Abraham, Isaac, and
    Jacob. In addition, what promised privilege did God offer
    to Israel, and what did he ask for in return? (See Exodus
    19:4 – 6; Deuteronomy 26:16 – 19.)

What had Israel done to earn this privileged status?

Why did God require Israel's obedience, and what level of
commitment did he expect?

4. Even when Israel disobeyed God, took his promises for
    granted or treated them lightly, and demonstrated disdain
    for being holy as he is holy, how did God continue to view
    them? (See Malachi 3:6 – 7, 16 – 18.)

What does this say to you about his forgiveness and enduring love?

Reflection

God made amazing promises concerning his chosen people, his
treasured possession. He delivered them from the cruel bondage of
Egypt and, on their journey through the desert to his mountain, carried them on his wings much like an eagle carries her young. If the
Israelites obeyed him, he would continue to care for them and honor

them as his holy people. Although we may not express them using the vivid images of the ancient Israelites, God gives similar promises to his people today (Titus 2:11 – 14; 1 Peter 2:4 – 12). By his grace, we too are his *segulah*!

Compare the promises of 1 Peter 2:4 – 12 to the ones Moses heard from God on Mount Sinai. (See Exodus 19:4 – 6; Deuteronomy 26:16 – 19.)

What similarities do you see between the defining statements and promises given to Israel and the defining statements and promises given to those who follow Jesus?

If you are a follower of Jesus, what do you think about who you are to God, and what have you done to earn your status?

Because of your status as *segulah* — a precious, living stone and part of God's holy priesthood and nation — do you think God desires from you the same commitment to obedience that he desired from the ancient Hebrews? Why or why not?

What is your response to God because he has made you his treasured possession? How willing are you to live in passionate obedience to his commands — to live such a good life that other people will see your good deeds and glorify God?

Where does your strength come from to partner with the Creator of the universe, and in what ways does the mother eagle metaphor help to portray this reality?

Memorize

As you come to him, the living Stone — rejected by men but chosen by God and precious to him — you also, like living stones, are being built into a spiritual house to be a holy priesthood, offering spiritual sacrifices acceptable to God through Jesus Christ.... You are a chosen people, a royal priesthood, a holy nation, a people belonging to God, that you may declare the praises of him who called you out of darkness into his wonderful light.

1 Peter 2:4 – 5, 9

Day Three | Recognizing the Presence of God

The Very Words of God

On the morning of the third day there was thunder and lightning, with a thick cloud over the mountain, and a very loud trumpet blast. Everyone in the camp trembled. Then Moses led the people out of the camp to meet with God, and they stood at the foot of the mountain. Mount Sinai was covered with smoke, because the LORD descended on it in fire. The smoke billowed up from it like smoke from a furnace, the whole mountain trembled violently, and the sound of the trumpet grew louder and louder. Then Moses spoke and the voice of God answered him.

Exodus 19:16 – 19

Bible Discovery

Fire as a Symbol of God's Presence

Imagine how the Israelites felt as they prepared for God to come down on Mount Sinai. They had seen God's power in the plagues and had followed his presence in the pillar of cloud and fire, but this was different. Now Moses told them that God was going to be "up close and personal" with them. He was going to come down in a dense cloud and speak to Moses so that they could hear him! They had washed their clothes, and Moses had consecrated them. They had been warned about getting too close to Mount Sinai, and limits had been placed around the mountain to protect them. What do you think they might have expected their encounter with God to be like?

1. What in the distant as well as recent history of the Israelites would have led them to recognize their God in the symbol of fire? (See Genesis 15:9 – 21; Exodus 13:20 – 22; 14:23 – 25.)

2. For what purposes did God speak to his people out of the fire on the mountain? (See Deuteronomy 4:10 – 12, 35 – 40.)

   What did the Israelites experience when Moses led them out of the camp to meet God at the foot of the mountain, and what impact did it have on them? (See Exodus 19:16 – 19.)

   How did the Israelites respond to having this close encounter with their God? How convinced were they that the Lord is God? (See Exodus 20:18 – 19; Deuteronomy 4:33; 5:1 – 5, 23 – 27.)

THINK ABOUT IT

How do you "see" thunder (Exodus 20:18)? According to a Jewish tradition from before Jesus' time, God's voice emerged from the fire on the mountain as tongues of fire. That detail is not in the biblical text, but it is certainly possible. Furthermore, the Hebrew word translated "thunder" can also be translated "languages," "tongues," or "voices." Clearly the concept of thunder, voices of tongues, and fire were significant in Israel's experience at Mount Sinai (as well as later at Pentecost in Jerusalem).

3. The physical nature of the fire of God is a frightening phenomenon by itself. But when you consider the fury and judgment of God that it can also symbolize, God's fire is truly terrifying. In what ways does your knowledge of God's fire in the following contexts add to the impact of how God appeared at Mount Sinai? (See Genesis 19:24 – 25; Isaiah 66:15 – 16; Malachi 3:2; Matthew 13:36 – 42; 2 Thessalonians 1:5 – 8; Revelation 20:7 – 10.)

4. Which future experiences of God's people would strengthen the Israelites' recognition that God used fire to represent his presence? (See Leviticus 9:22 – 24; 10:1 – 2; Numbers 9:15 – 16; 11:1 – 3; 1 Kings 18:20 – 38; 2 Chronicles 7:1 – 3.)

5. When God uses fire to signify his presence, which characteristics of his nature is he often communicating? (See Exodus 3:1 – 5; 24:17; Leviticus 2:1 – 3; 21:6; 2 Chronicles 7:1- 3; Isaiah 4:5; 10:17.)

What, then, might be the significance of God using fire to symbolize his presence when he spoke the Ten Commandments to Moses?

DID YOU REALIZE?

The parallels between the formative events the Israelites experienced at Mount Sinai and the formative events the early Christian believers experienced at Pentecost are significant:

The Hebrews (Israel) left Egypt on the fourteenth day of the first month — celebrated by the holiday of Passover (Exodus 12:6, 12; Leviticus 23). Jesus died on Passover.

After traveling just over forty days (about fourteen days in the first month and twenty-eight days in the second month) Israel reached Mount Sinai on the first day of the third month and Moses went up to God (Exodus 19:1–3). Jesus went to the Mount of Olives and ascended to heaven forty days after Passover (Acts 1:1–12; Luke 24:50–53).

Around Pentecost (*Shavuoth*), when Israel was at Mount Sinai, God gave the Ten Commandments to instruct his people in how to obey him. On Pentecost, God gave his Spirit to instruct the early followers of Jesus in how to live for him.

NOTE: God spoke the Ten Commandments very near the festival of *Shavuoth*, which is a celebration of the wheat harvest, a main source of bread for the Hebrews. So perhaps it is not surprising that Moses wrote, "Man does not live on bread alone but on every word that comes from the mouth of the LORD" (Deuteronomy 8:3). It makes sense that if man does not live by bread alone, for which *Shavuoth* was the festival of thanksgiving, God would reveal the words that his people do need to live by — the Ten Commandments — on the same day.

Reflection

The stories about God's presence at Mount Sinai and at Pentecost after Jesus' ascension to heaven are much more than events in the history of God's ancient people. These stories remind us of God's holiness, glory, majesty ... and our challenge to respond to him accordingly. They reveal more of God's great redemptive plan that he continues in Jesus and in us! The question for us is, do we value what happened at Sinai as being relevant to us?

Think for a moment about what God wanted his people to learn during the time they spent at Mount Sinai.

Have we learned the lessons they learned, failed as they failed, and can we learn from those failures?

Are the things they experienced and learned as foundational to our Christian walk as they were to the Israelites?

What value do you see in being able to say, as Jewish people do today, "we" were at Sinai and "we" heard God's voice?

How do you experience the holiness and glory of God?

Which symbol of God's presence might help you to reclaim some of the impact of the concrete images God used to demonstrate his presence to the ancient Israelites?

Which specific things will you do in order to cultivate and maintain a sense of God's power, presence, awesome holiness, and justice as you live your life before him?

At Sinai, the people asked Moses to speak to them for God, and some followers of Jesus essentially do the same today. They want someone else to speak for God — to teach them his Word and tell them what it means or what God wants — rather than learning from God directly.

What do you see as the advantages and disadvantages of doing this in your walk with God?

Which do you desire most — to stand a "safe" distance from the thunder and fire of God's presence, or to be like Moses who wouldn't miss the opportunity to experience God to the fullest? Why?

FOR GREATER UNDERSTANDING

Great parallels exist between the presence of God at Mount Sinai, when he gave the Hebrews the Torah, and his presence at Pentecost, when he gave his Spirit to the new believers after Jesus' ascension to heaven. Because God used the same dramatic portrayal of his presence in Jerusalem that he had used in stunning ways at Mount Sinai, Jewish people who were participating in the festival knew that what they were witnessing represented God's presence.

On Mount Sinai	During Pentecost
Fire, smoke, and the sound of thunder accompanied God's presence (Ex. 19:16–19).	God's presence was accompanied by a sound like wind, tongues of fire, and the gift of languages that in Hebrew is the same word translated as "thunder" (Acts 2:1–4). The Hebrew term translated "Holy Spirit," *Ruach HaKodesh*, means "holy wind."
God's presence was symbolized by a cloud and fire, which led the Israelites out of Egypt. Later, God moved his presence into the temple (2 Chron. 5:7–8, 13–14).	God's presence, evident in rushing wind and tongues of fire, moved from the temple into a new "temple"—followers of Jesus (Rom. 8:9; 1 Cor. 3:16–17).
God met Moses—the Israelites' leader—on Mount Sinai, "the mountain of God" (Ex. 24:13).	Jerusalem was built on a mountain called "the mountain of the LORD" (Isa. 2:3).
Shortly after God gave Moses the Torah, the people worshiped the golden calf. About 3,000 people died as punishment for their sins (Ex. 32:1–4, 19–20, 27–28).[1]	When Jesus' Spirit was given, many people repented and about 3,000 believed and found spiritual life in God (Acts 2:41).
The Torah (*Torah* means "teaching") provided God's teachings for the Old Testament community of God's people.	The Holy Spirit became the Teacher of believers (John 14:26).

To further explore this important connection between Mount Sinai and Pentecost, please see session 9, "Power to the People" of *Faith Lessons on the Death and Resurrection of the Messiah* (Faith Lessons vol. 4).

Day Four | Enthroning God as King

The Very Words of God

> *Now if you obey me fully and keep my covenant, then out of all nations*
> *you will be my treasured possession. Although the whole earth is mine,*
> *you will be for me a kingdom of priests and a holy nation.*

> *Exodus 19:5 – 6*

Bible Discovery

If You Obey Me Fully . . .

God made a covenant with Abraham more than four hundred years
before Israel stood at Mount Sinai and received his gift of the Torah.
He promised Abraham that his descendants would be God's chosen people forever and that he would bless them for Abraham's
sake — and bless the entire world through them. Now that God
had redeemed his people from slavery and led them to his mountain, it was time for them to take a more active role in his plan. If
they became active participants in God's kingdom by obeying his
every word, they would become his kingdom of priests and his holy
nation, and the world would be blessed by the shalom (order, harmony) they brought to it. God did not demand obedience from the
Israelites as a precondition for their redemption from slavery; they
were already God's people. He demanded their obedience because
the future direction of his kingdom depended on whether or not
they would enthrone him as their Lord and King.

FOR GREATER UNDERSTANDING
The Progression of God's Kingdom

Text	God's Kingdom: From Shalom to Enthroning God as King[2]
Gen. 1	God the sovereign Creator brought order (shalom) out of chaos.
Gen. 3–4, 11	Sin began to return God's beautiful order into chaos. Chaos, seen first in individuals, then grew to become communities and kingdoms that were opposed to God's order.
Gen. 12, 15	God revealed his plan to destroy chaos and restore shalom.
Ex. 1–3	God's people were enslaved in Egypt, at the mercy of a kingdom of chaos.
Ex. 7–12 (8:19)	God's eternal kingdom—his reign and restoration of shalom—began when he used his "finger" to act powerfully against the evil in Egypt that brought chaos into the lives of his people.
Ex. 15:2–3, 18	Having witnessed God's powerful "finger" at work, Israel danced for joy at the Red Sea and professed that the Lord reigns forever. In faith, they acknowledged him as their reigning King, which means his kingdom has been established.
Ex. 19:3–8	At the mountain of God, Israel—individually and corporately—chose to "enthrone him" as their reigning King by committing themselves to obey him. Thus they became participants in his kingdom.

1. After freeing the Hebrews from Egyptian slavery, destroying Pharaoh's army, dividing the Red Sea, and providing for Israel in the desert, where did God lead the Israelites and what was his purpose for taking them there? (See Exodus 19:1–6.)

What might Israel have seen and experienced thus far in their journey with God that would make accepting their role in his kingdom and his requirements for obedience more compelling?

DID YOU KNOW?

If you were to ask an Orthodox rabbi when and where the kingdom of heaven (kingdom of God) first appears in the Bible, he would say it was when the Hebrews first praised their God who is reigning forever. Although it is true that from Genesis forward the Bible describes God as the Creator and sovereign Lord of all, it is in Exodus that God displays his great power to redeem a people who then acknowledge his lordship and reign. Out of all the nations on earth, the Hebrews were the first to accept God's reign in their lives. God then desired that they would become a living example of his reign and the shalom it brings so that other nations would also enthrone God in their lives and cultures.

2. How did the Israelites respond to God's call for obedient participation in his kingdom? (See Exodus 19:8; 24:3 – 4, 7; Deuteronomy 5:27.)

Are you willing to say to God, "Everything you command I will do"? Why or why not?

3. When God promised his redeemed people that if they obeyed him they would be a "kingdom of priests and a holy nation" (Exodus 19:6), what do you understand that to mean?

FOR GREATER UNDERSTANDING
To Be God's Kingdom of Priests

When God stated his desire for Israel to be his "kingdom of priests and a holy nation," the Israelites viewed their position to be that of a servant nation, not a ruling nation. Their amazing purpose was to serve God as his priests—to present him, represent him, and display him to the world—and thereby bless all nations. In a real sense, they were to be God's holy partners in bringing shalom—peace, order, purpose, harmony—to a broken, defiant world and in drawing it back into relationship to God. They were to be a holy people among all people, and their obedience would make them a kingdom of priests. Sinai was the beginning of God's cosmic drama of reconciliation, ushered in when Israel chose to be participants in God's kingdom. Through their obedience, the Israelites enthroned God as their King.

As God taught and prepared the Israelites to be his holy nation, they had little understanding of their mission and how difficult it would be to keep God's condition: "if you obey me." Despite setbacks, God's kingdom continued to flourish. Later, Jesus the Messiah dramatically advanced the kingdom by feeding the hungry, healing the sick, casting out demons, loving the weak, and restoring the dispossessed. And he instructed his disciples in how to participate in God's kingdom: "Go and make disciples of all nations, baptizing . . . , teaching them to obey everything I have commanded you" (Matthew 28:19–20). When he died for the sins of the world and rose from the dead, he overcame the greatest chaos of all—death. How well do we, as followers of Jesus who also have been given priestly duties, understand our mission?

THE KINGDOM OF HEAVEN

People obey:
God enthroned as their King

He is reigning:
People call him Lord

Finger of God: God acts with power

Kingdom of heaven

Yahweh destroying
power of evil

Yahweh restoring his
creation (shalom)

This diagram indicates the fullness of the kingdom of heaven. God created the world out of chaos, and sin brought chaos back to his world. God's redemptive plan is based on two ongoing actions: defeating the chaos and the evil one behind it, and bringing shalom to a broken world. God could do this himself, but he has partnered with fallen humanity to restore his kingdom. That restored shalom is identified as the kingdom of heaven in Jewish thought.

The kingdom comes with three elements:

1. Human strength cannot bring the kingdom, for it must begin with the power of God, the "finger of God" as identified by the Egyptians (Exodus 8:19).
2. When God acts with power, the response of his people is to call him their Lord or King as the Hebrews did at the Red Sea (Exodus 15:18).
3. God demands that those who call him Lord enthrone him as the King of their lives by obedience — a demand he reveals to Moses at Mount Sinai (Exodus 19:5 – 6).

Jesus uses the same language to describe the coming of the kingdom of heaven in his teaching: "But if I drive out demons by the finger of God, then the kingdom of God has come upon you" (Luke 11:20) and "Not everyone who says to me, 'Lord, Lord,' will enter the kingdom of heaven, but only those who do the will of my Father who is in heaven" (Matthew 7:21).

4. We know that God's ongoing purpose for his chosen people
    was to bless all peoples on earth (Genesis 12:1 – 3). What are
    some ways other people will be blessed when God's people
    obey his commands? (See Deuteronomy 4:5 – 8; Psalm 67;
    Isaiah 2:1 – 5; 56:3 – 8; Zechariah 8:20 – 23.)

5. Because of God's love for his chosen people, what did he
    provide to guide and instruct them so they could choose to
    live his way in obedience and experience a full, vibrant life?
    (See Deuteronomy 7:7 – 11; 30:11 – 20.)

The Torah, or "law" as Christians often call it, is sometimes
thought to be an unbearable burden that God's chosen
people simply couldn't bear. To the Hebrew mind, however,
the Torah is a gift of instruction and guidance. In what ways
does the psalmist's view of God's teaching give you a new
perspective on the Torah? (See Psalm 19:7 – 8; 119:97 – 104,
162 – 168.)

FOR GREATER UNDERSTANDING

The Torah: God's Gift

Christians often refer to the Torah as "the law," but the Hebrew word *Torah*
actually means "teaching." Although it is true that the Torah comprises many
"laws," that designation has led to a negative perception of it in the minds
of some people, which is not how God's people viewed it. The Hebrew root

of Torah, *yarah*, means "to show the way, to teach, to guide, to instruct." Thus Torah might best be thought of as a gift of God's loving instruction that guided his already redeemed people in how to live his way.

That's why religious Jews find such delight in the Torah. It is not an oppressive burden. Rather, it might be compared to the kind of instruction loving parents give their children in order to show them how to live a vibrant, full life.[3] That is why the Torah includes so much more than "laws." It tells about creation; the flood; Abraham, Isaac, and Jacob; the exodus; the tabernacle; the priesthood; manna. It tells wonderful stories of God loving his people and their struggle to be faithful to him. It gives examples of God's grace, justice, and judgment against sin.

God did not demand obedience to the Torah as a precondition for his redemption of the Israelites. He had already redeemed them by his grace. Obedience to Torah simply enabled the Israelites to know how to obey God and fulfill their calling to be a kingdom of priests and a people who would be a witness to the world that God desired to redeem (Exodus 19:2 – 6).

Reflection

To participate in the kingdom of God is to recognize the "little finger" of God's mighty power at work against the suffering brought by chaos, to acknowledge his reign over all creation, and to enthrone him as King by obeying his commands. God is sovereign Lord over everything that is, and he reigns over nations that do not even know him. God called the Israelites to a life of passionate obedience because he wanted them to be the nation of priests who would help other nations know him.

The kingdom of God theme is central to the message of the Christian Testament just as it is to the Hebrew Testament. It was the theme of John the Baptist (Matthew 3:2), Jesus and his disciples (Matthew 9:35; 10:7, Luke 9:1 - 2), and Paul (Acts 19:8).

So how does God's challenge to the Israelites to live as his priests in their world relate to those of us who follow Jesus today?

Are you willing, as Moses challenged the ancient Hebrews, to say to God that "everything he commands you will do"? Why or why not?

What is involved in being a holy "priest" of God — that is, a person who displays God to others through obedience to his commands?

What is the implication for you of displaying God's holiness in every aspect of life, presenting God every moment so that your family, friends, neighbors, faith community members, employees, coworkers, and even total strangers ... see God (Jesus) in you? Which change(s) might you need to make in order to live this way?

Sometimes people in Western cultures focus so intently on their individual relationship with God that they forget that his great desire is for all nations and peoples to know (experience) him. God selects human "priests" to present and display him. Who misses out if God's people are not holy as he is holy?

For which reasons, then, is God angered when his people disobey him? Is it only because he hates sin and demands righteousness, or are there other reasons?

Why do you think some people who speak dramatically about their belief in God do not seem to obey their sovereign King even in routine, ordinary situations, and what is the impact of this behavior?

What have we lost sight of that allows obedience to God to receive so little emphasis among most people today?

What can you do, individually and corporately, to begin to regain what has been lost?

How "hungry" are you to study God's Word and learn how to obey him? Where would you start — the Torah, the Gospels? Why?

Day Five | Moses Kept Climbing the Mountain

The Very Words of God

> *The LORD descended to the top of Mount Sinai and called Moses to the top of the mountain. So Moses went up.*

> *Exodus 19:20*

Bible Discovery

Follow God with All Your Might

When Moses reached Mount Sinai, he was at least eighty years old. He had been a shepherd for forty years, he had courageously challenged Pharaoh during the time of plagues, and he had faced the Israelites' unbelief, anger, rebellion, disobedience, and fear in the desert. But when Israel arrived at the mountain of God, there is a sense in which his work was just beginning! Moses faced new challenges at Mount Sinai, including climbing up and down the mountain multiple times! Notice how much effort Moses put into obeying God.

1. As soon as Moses arrived at Mount Sinai, he began the first of many trips up the mountain to meet with God (Exodus 19:1 – 6). Remember the video and the scenes of the climb up Jebel Katarina? Although some proposed locations for Mount Sinai are less of a climb than this one (others are more), all are quite steep. Any of them would be an exhausting climb for an eighty-year-old man. What does this say to you about the effort God expects from his people, and in what ways must God have provided for Moses?

**NO MATTER WHICH MOUNTAIN MOSES CLIMBED, IT REQUIRED SIG-
NIFICANT EFFORT ON HIS PART. IMAGINE CLIMBING UP AND DOWN
THESE MOUNTAINS SEVERAL TIMES IN A SHORT PERIOD OF TIME!**

2. Take the time to read the following record of Moses' trips
   up and down Mount Sinai. Note what took place, the effort
   Moses put into each encounter with God, what God was
   communicating, and the impact these treks were having on
   Moses and his knowledge (experience) of God.

Text	Up and Down the Mountain
Ex. 19:3–8	How long would it take to read this message in comparison to how long it took to obtain it?
Ex. 19:8–14	How long do you think this communication took?
Ex. 19:20–25	What was the first thing God asked when Moses reached the top of the mountain?
Ex. 20:18–21	Why do you think Moses was unafraid to approach God when the people were afraid even to hear his voice?
Exodus 24:1–11	What did God provide for Moses and the elders during this trip up the mountain?

continued on next page . . .

Text	Up and Down the Mountain
Ex. 24:12–18	How long did Moses stay on the mountain?
Ex. 32:7–20; Deut. 9:18	How long did Moses stay on the mountain, and what was he doing on behalf of the people?
Ex. 34:1–5, 28	What did Moses carry up the mountain on this trip, and how long did he stay there?
Deut. 34:1–12	What is the message of Moses' life, and how did climbing Mount Nebo on the day he died help illustrate it?

NOTE: All of these climbs occurred within a relatively short time frame — some within a few days. If you have not been in the desert mountains of the Sinai Peninsula to experience the rough, steep terrain and the heat of the day and cold of the night, it is difficult to imagine the huge effort Moses put into meeting with God.

3. God promised that another prophet like Moses would come one day (Deuteronomy 18:15, 17-18; John 6:14; Acts 3:17-22; Hebrews 3:1-5). The following verses contain amazing parallels between Moses and Jesus. Review each one and note what each reveals about (1) Moses being a paradigm of Jesus; (2) Jesus' commitment to obeying the Hebrew Bible (Romans 5:19; Hebrews 5:8-9; 4:15); and (3) Jesus' living his life so that it was shaped by biblical stories and commands.

Moses—Prophet for People of the Exodus	Jesus the Messiah
Ex. 1:15–16; 2:1–3— situation at birth	Matt. 2:13—situation at birth
Ex. 15:20—name of sister	Luke 2:1–5—(In Hebrew, "Mary" is "Miriam.")

Moses—Prophet for People of the Exodus	Jesus the Messiah
Ex. 12—gave God's revelation that shaped this last plague event in Egypt	John 1:29–30; Luke 22:13–19— what Jesus was, and how he reframed the Lord's Supper in light of this.
Acts 7:29–30; Deut. 29:5	Matt. 4:1–2
Deut. 8:3; 6:16; 6:13	Matt. 4:4, 7, 10
Ex. 34:27–28	Matt. 4:1–2
Ex. 24:4	Matt. 10:1
Ex.19:1–3—Moses received central revelation from God here.	Matt. 5:1—Jesus delivered central revelation here.
Exodus 16:11–15, 31	John 6:32–35
Num. 21:4–9	John 3:14–15
Ex. 32:31–32	John 3:16

continued on next page . . .

Moses—Prophet for People of the Exodus	Jesus the Messiah
Ex. 24:15–16	Matt. 17:1–5; Luke 9:29–30

What did you learn as you compared aspects of Moses' life with the life of Jesus? Why are these points important?

Reflection

It's not easy for most of us to realize just how much effort Moses expended for God and how much he needed to receive from God in order to fulfill his calling. God expected an unbelievable effort in serving him, yet all the strength to do what he commanded — to accomplish those tasks — came from him as a gift. Today, each of us faces a different, yet similar, situation. Will we strive to obey God passionately in all areas of life and rely on him for whatever we need to live for him? Remember, to demonstrate love for God is to obey his commandments. God's blessings await everyone who pursues this kind of relationship with him!

Why do you think God demanded that Moses demonstrate such a deep level of obedient commitment?

What level of commitment has God required of you?

What if Moses, after recognizing that ultimately his strength had to come from God, had stopped giving God everything he had to give? What if Moses had said, "I'm too old to climb mountains"?

When is realizing the scriptural truth that a relationship with God is by grace alone sometimes used as an excuse for expending little effort toward obedience?

How would you compare the level of effort you have expended in order to be faithful to God in light of the effort Moses made — including his physically demanding treks up and down Mount Sinai?

Which specific steps might you take to increase your level of commitment in order to give God all that you have?

When have you, or someone you know, given every ounce you had in order to overcome a difficult situation and then later realized that God had sustained you every moment? Share that experience with someone.

Memorize

> *When a prophet of the LORD is among you,*
> > *I reveal myself to him in visions,*
> > *I speak to him in dreams.*
> *But this is not true of my servant Moses;*
> > *he is faithful in all my house.*
> *With him I speak face to face,*
> > *clearly and not in riddles;*
> > *he sees the form of the LORD.*

Numbers 12:6 – 8

I LED YOU LIKE A BRIDE: A WEDDING AT SINAI

Exodus 19–20, 24

What could God possibly have wanted with a tribe of Hebrews enslaved in Egypt? Why did God redeem them and guide them across the hostile wilderness (while they seem to have complained all the way) to the mountain called by his name — the mountain of God? If ever there was an unlikely plot for a true story, this has to be it.

As we explored in the last session, God used this opportunity to give the Torah to Moses at Mount Sinai. The Torah was the revelation of what the Creator of the universe desired from his people. It became the foundation of a moral and legal system that continues — although not without constant attack — to this day. Did God simply desire to create a legal/moral system that he provided for the world? Or was there something more?

A careful study of Scripture reveals the astonishing truth that the Creator was unfolding his plan to come down from heaven, establish an intimate and loving relationship with his people, and live with them! God was like a husband looking for a deep and personal relationship with his bride, longing for a partnership with the people he had chosen. And the Ten Commandments, the legal system he provided, summarized their covenant and spelled out how he loved them and how his people could express their love for him.

Although the Israelites deserved or earned none of his love and mercy, God still redeemed them. By his grace alone, he brought them out of Egypt and across the desert. As they grumbled and resisted his ways, he demonstrated the kind of husband he would be by his patience, protection, and provision, but even that was not enough. He declared to Moses that he wanted to take these people and bring them to himself as a husband would embrace his wife (Exodus 6:7 – 8; 19:4). Seen in this light, the history of Israel is an amazing love story in which God loved the Hebrew people far more than they loved him. It is the unfolding story of the relationship between the always faithful God and his sometimes faithless people.

At Sinai, God established a covenant relationship with his people. This made their relationship more than a temporary liaison, more than a legal or political union. It created a relationship that, at its heart, implied a marriage, and Mount Sinai was where the wedding would take place. God had planned and prepared everything — the *mikveh*, the *chuppah*, the *ketubah*, the Sabbath — a bridal chamber where he would meet regularly with his bride. And as we'll see, even the language God used on his mountain did not reflect the cold demands of a legal system but rather the tender language of intimate love. The covenant God established with his people resembled a marriage so closely that later prophets described it in those terms.

By his love, God singled out Israel and those who would join her as his people (Deuteronomy 10:12 – 15). For the sake of that love, he gave the Torah to Moses to give to Israel. The Ten Commandments that summarized the "laws" and the covenant were the love language God's people were to use to show their passion for him. In fact, the love he showed his chosen people as they left Egypt, came to his mountain, and continued their journey into the Promised Land would become the metaphor for the love between a man and a woman in marriage.

Eventually, God's desire for an intimate relationship with his bride would lead him to become one of us! Through what Jesus, the bridegroom, accomplished for humankind, God would provide for his bride what they could never provide for themselves: the holy and pure character that the husband desires. Thus the wedding at Sinai not only shaped the relationship between God and his people, it had a part in God's eternal plan to redeem his world and restore shalom.

Let's go to Mount Sinai to attend the wedding of God and his people!

Opening Thoughts (3 minutes)

The Very Words of God

> *I remember the devotion of your youth, how as a bride you loved me and followed me through the desert, through a land not sown.*

> *Jeremiah 2:2*

Think About It

The story of God giving the Ten Commandments to Israel at Mount Sinai is probably one of the best-known accounts in the Bible. Even people who don't know what all of the commandments are or why God gave them at least have heard of them.

How much thought have you given to understanding God's greater purpose in guiding his chosen people to Mount Sinai? What do you think God wanted to accomplish in the hearts of his people? What part do you think giving them the Torah had in his overall purpose for their lives and for the restoration of shalom to his world?

DVD Notes (27 minutes)

Mount Sinai as a wedding

The Ten Commandments as wedding vows

An affair at the wedding!

God's forgiveness

Obedience, the language of love

DVD Discussion (6 minutes)

1.　If we think of the covenant made between God and Israel at Mount Sinai as a wedding, then the previous six or so weeks was a courtship. What a courtship it was!

On the map of Lower Egypt and the Sinai Peninsula, locate Goshen, the region where the Israelites are likely to have crossed the sea, the Desert of Sin, Rephidim, and Jebel Katarina and Jebel Musa in southern Sinai. As you trace Israel's journey and locate the general areas where the video was filmed, remember what happened at each place we have studied in terms of God courting his bride, Israel. (Again, these sites represent the places mentioned in the Bible and are not meant to be thought of as exact locations.)

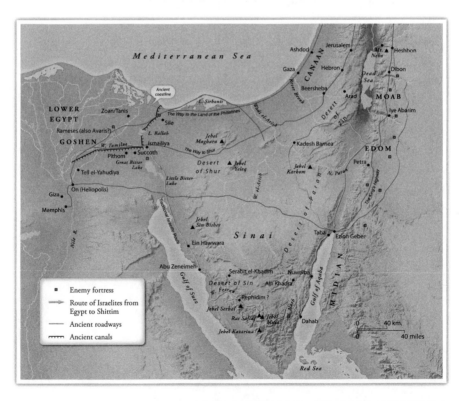

LOWER EGYPT AND THE SINAI PENINSULA

Take a fresh look at the following events as being God's courtship of Israel. Remember:

- How the Hebrews eagerly marched out of Egypt
- The Israelites' dreadful fear (before) and overwhelming joy (after) at the crossing of the sea
- The bitter complaining at Marah
- The refreshing days at Elim
- The ungrateful longing for Egypt's food
- God's gift of manna
- How God provided water at Rephidim
- The attack and battle against the Amalekites
- At last, arriving at Mount Sinai

Would you have loved the bridegroom who "carried you on his wings" through all of this? Why or why not?

What about that bride? Might you have had some concerns about her? Why or why not?

2. In what ways does viewing God's interaction with the Israelites at Mount Sinai as a wedding — as God "taking" his people, Israel, to be his bride — change your view of the whole account?

In what ways is this a new perspective for you to consider?

Does it make sense to you? Why or why not?

THINK ABOUT IT

The Hebrew word *laqakh* describes the action of taking a wife for oneself, or taking a wife for another person. God used this word to describe bringing Israel to himself. Consider the following passages in which *laqakh* is used: Genesis 4:19; 11:29; 12:19; 21:21; 24:4, 7, 40, 48; 25:1, 20; Exodus 2:1; 6:6 – 7; Jeremiah 29:6.

3. In what ways does viewing the Mount Sinai event as a wedding give you a different picture not only of the event itself, but of God's view of the *chuppah* (covering), *mikveh* (consecration), *ketubah* (Ten Commandments), and Sabbath (the sign of the covenant)?

   Which of these become more meaningful and/or important to you in light of the wedding perspective? Why?

4. In what ways does the wedding perspective help you to better know (experience) what God must have felt when his people worshiped the golden calf? Why?

Small Group Bible Discovery and Discussion (17 minutes)

Marriage at Mount Sinai? The Testimony of the Text

Jewish people believe that the meeting between God and Israel at Mount Sinai, when he gave the Torah, is a marriage. Although the historical event does not specifically describe God's revelation as a wedding, the relationship between God and Israel as revealed on Mount Sinai came in the form of a covenant. It is clear that Israel, as well as God's inspired prophets, viewed the Mount Sinai covenant as being like a marriage. So let's consider the biblical evidence for a marriage covenant at Sinai.

1. With whom had God made a covenant long before the exodus, and for how long was it to be in force? (See Genesis 17:1 – 9.)

   What promises and requirements were included in that covenant, and for whom? (See Exodus 19:3 – 6.)

   On the basis of the covenant he had made with Abraham, what did God decide to do concerning the Hebrew slaves? (See Exodus 6:2 – 8.)

   How many years had passed since God made his covenant with Abraham, and what does this say to you about God's character? (See Exodus 12:40 – 41.)

> **DID YOU KNOW?**
>
> A "covenant" is an agreement between two parties in which both promise under oath to perform or refrain from certain actions described in advance. Covenants were common in the ancient Near Eastern cultures of the Bible. When two parties made a covenant, each party normally took a summary copy of the covenant and placed it in their most sacred place, where it would be read regularly as a reminder of the covenant.
>
> The covenant was a major metaphor in the Scriptures describing the relationship between God and his people. Following the typical custom, God instructed Moses to make two summary documents of the covenant God had made with his people. These documents (each of which contained all Ten Commandments) were his guarantee that his word would never fail. God, however, gave both copies to Moses and ordered him to place them into the ark of the covenant. This indicated that God's most sacred place was the same as Israel's most sacred place. It was God's way of saying that he would dwell with his chosen people.

2. How do we know that God was making a new covenant with Israel at Mount Sinai? (See Exodus 24:3 – 8, 12; 32:15 – 16; 34:10 – 11; Deuteronomy 4:9 – 14; 5:1 – 3; 2 Chronicles 5:10.)

    What were the promises and commands of this covenant?

3. The later prophets who spoke for God shed light on what kind of covenant God made with his people at Mount Sinai. In the following passages, what do you think are the implications in the prophets' testimony that God viewed the Mount

Sinai experience as establishing a marriage covenant with his people?

a.   *Jeremiah 2:1 - 7.* What language did Jeremiah use to describe what Israel was to God as he led her out of Egypt and across the desert? What accusation did Jeremiah make against Israel?

b.   *Hosea 2:14 - 16, 19 - 20.* What language did Hosea use to describe God's desired relationship with Israel? What does God desire from Israel?

c.   *Jeremiah 31:31 - 33.* What was God to Israel as a result of the covenant made at Mount Sinai? Why was a new covenant necessary?

FOR GREATER UNDERSTANDING
The Sinai Marriage Covenant

Marriage was one of many types of ancient covenants, which were agreements in which each party committed to fulfill a set of obligations to the other party. In Scripture, marriage is viewed as a covenant relationship. In Malachi 2:13 – 14, God addressed the unfaithfulness of his people, Israel, in terms of breaking faith with the partner of their marriage covenant.

So, was the agreement between God and his people at Mount Sinai a marriage covenant? Apparently it was. God chose to describe his relationship to his people using a significant word picture — that of a husband to a wife. The betrothal — the commitment to marriage — was the giving of the Torah on Mount Sinai. In the language of ancient covenant making, this marriage relationship was not based as much on the emotional attachment of love as is the case in Western culture; it was based on the intimate bond of a covenant commitment. A trace of this ancient practice may still be seen in Jewish wedding ceremonies in which the *ketubah,* or marriage contract, is read.

We do not yet know what the ancient Israelites' wedding rituals were like. Whether God patterned what happened at Mount Sinai to be similar to the cultural rituals, or whether the Mount Sinai events shaped the Israelites' rituals, it is clear that the people understood the momentous events of that experience to be a betrothal between God and his people—that is, a husband and his bride. From this perspective, the events of Mount Sinai reveal an intimacy and depth of love that is seldom considered in the Western world, which tends to focus on the legal nature of God's revelation of the Torah. This may help to explain why Jews who clearly recognize the significance of the legal code given in the Torah are also deeply moved by the relationship God established with his people at Mount Sinai.

4. In what way(s) has your understanding of the Ten Commandments and what God wanted to accomplish by giving them to Israel changed as a result of this study?

What difference will what you have learned make in your relationship with God, and why?

Faith Lesson (5 minutes)

In session 4, we explored how God considered his chosen people to be his *segulah* — his treasured possession — his kingdom of priests and holy nation. We saw how God intended Israel to obey him and live such holy lives that all the nations would come to know him. In the making of his covenant with Israel at Mount Sinai, we begin to see the more intimate side of God's exclusive relationship with his *segulah*: a relationship that later biblical writers would describe as a marriage. What an amazing picture this perspective provides of the Creator's passionate love for his bride! By establishing his covenant with Israel, God in a sense was saying that Israel would always be his beloved. But to experience that love, Israel would have to maintain that covenant relationship with him by faithfully obeying, following, and living as his bride. (See Exodus 19:5.)

1. What have you come to know (experience) regarding God's love for his people, Israel, through your exploration of the wedding event at Mount Sinai?

   What have you learned about God's heart of love through the tenderness, faithfulness, and care he expressed to his bride, Israel (during his desert courtship and in making his covenant)? What does this mean to you?

   As you think about the Ten Commandments, the summary document of the covenant between God and Israel (see pages 210–211), how would obedience to these commands help an unworthy bride to respond appropriately to the love of her husband and bring honor to him through their relationship?

   What has been your personal experience in seeing the connection between your obedience to God and the depth of intimacy you have in your relationship with him?

2. God chose and redeemed his people on the basis of his covenant with Abraham and his love for them — not on the basis of Israel's status, accomplishments, strength, intelligence, beauty, or hard work. In a similar way, God chooses and redeems people today on the basis of his love and grace as shown through the shed blood of his son, Jesus Christ. Writers of the Christian Testament have made it clear that those who commit themselves to following Jesus also are God's *segulah* and become part of the people "belonging to God."

Compare the word pictures Peter used for God's people (1 Peter 2:9) to those used in God's revelation to Moses (Exodus 19:5 – 6; Deuteronomy 7:6).

1 Peter 2:9	Exodus 19:5–6 and Deuteronomy 7:6
A chosen people	The Lord your God has chosen you
A holy nation	A holy nation
A royal priesthood	A kingdom of priests
A people belonging to God	His treasured possession

Do you see that if you follow Jesus the Messiah, you also are God's treasured possession, part of God's people going back to the exodus and before? What does this mean to you?

How much do you want to demonstrate your love (obedience) toward God because he has chosen you to be his treasured bride and you are delighted to belong to him?

In what specific ways do you show your love to God every day?

3. Consider how much the language of the apostle Paul in 2 Corinthians 11:2–3 sounds like that used at Mount Sinai: "I promised you to one husband, to Christ, so that I might present you as a pure virgin to him. But I am afraid that just as Eve was deceived by the serpent's cunning, your minds may somehow be led astray from your sincere and pure devotion to Christ."

In what ways does this language open your eyes to God's desire for a more personal, intimate relationship with you?

How does your perspective on obedience to God's commands change if you see them as an expression of "sincere and pure devotion" rather than a legalistic list of dos and don'ts?

What is your desire and commitment to obey God's commands, and what changes will you make to obey God in every aspect of life?

Closing (2 minutes)

Read the Ten Commandments aloud together (Exodus 20:1–17). Read them not just as a list of dos and don'ts but as God's passionate declaration of love to you.

And God spoke all these words:

"I am the LORD your God, who brought you out of Egypt, out of the land of slavery.

"You shall have no other gods before me.

"You shall not make for yourself an idol in the form of anything in heaven above or on the earth beneath or in the waters below. You shall not bow down to them or worship them; for I, the Lord your God, am a jealous God, punishing the children for the sin of the fathers to the third and fourth generation of those who hate me, but showing love to a thousand generations of those who love me and keep my commandments.

"You shall not misuse the name of the Lord your God, for the Lord will not hold anyone guiltless who misuses his name.

"Remember the Sabbath day by keeping it holy. Six days you shall labor and do all your work, but the seventh day is a Sabbath to the Lord your God. On it you shall not do any work, neither you, nor your son or daughter, nor your manservant or maidservant, nor your animals, nor the alien within your gates. For in six days the Lord made the heavens and the earth, the sea, and all that is in them, but he rested on the seventh day. Therefore the Lord blessed the Sabbath day and made it holy.

"Honor your father and your mother, so that you may live long in the land the Lord your God is giving you.

"You shall not murder.

"You shall not commit adultery.

"You shall not steal.

"You shall not give false testimony against your neighbor.

"You shall not covet your neighbor's house. You shall not covet your neighbor's wife, or his manservant or maidservant, his ox or donkey, or anything that belongs to your neighbor."

Thank God for his love for you and ask him for the passion and strength to be a faithful, obedient bride — a holy *segulah* for him.

Memorize

And God spoke all these words:

"I am the Lord your God, who brought you out of Egypt, out of the land of slavery.

"You shall have no other gods before me.

"You shall not make for yourself an idol in the form of anything in heaven above or on the earth beneath or in the waters below. You shall not bow down to them or worship them; for I, the Lord your God, am a jealous God, punishing the children for the sin of the fathers to

the third and fourth generation of those who hate me, but showing love to a thousand generations of those who love me and keep my commandments.

"You shall not misuse the name of the L<small>ORD</small> *your God, for the* L<small>ORD</small> *will not hold anyone guiltless who misuses his name.*

"Remember the Sabbath day by keeping it holy. Six days you shall labor and do all your work, but the seventh day is a Sabbath to the L<small>ORD</small> *your God. On it you shall not do any work, neither you, nor your son or daughter, nor your manservant or maidservant, nor your animals, nor the alien within your gates. For in six days the* L<small>ORD</small> *made the heavens and the earth, the sea, and all that is in them, but he rested on the seventh day. Therefore the* L<small>ORD</small> *blessed the Sabbath day and made it holy.*

"Honor your father and your mother, so that you may live long in the land the L<small>ORD</small> *your God is giving you.*

"You shall not murder.

"You shall not commit adultery.

"You shall not steal.

"You shall not give false testimony against your neighbor.

"You shall not covet your neighbor's house. You shall not covet your neighbor's wife, or his manservant or maidservant, his ox or donkey, or anything that belongs to your neighbor."

Exodus 20:1 – 17

Tested and Trained to Be God's Message

In-Depth Personal Study Sessions

Day One | God Prepares His Bride, Israel

The Very Words of God

> *As a bridegroom rejoices over his bride, so will your God rejoice over you.*
>
> Isaiah 62:5

Bible Discovery

God Courts Israel in the Desert

If the wedding of God and his bride, Israel, occurred at Mount Sinai, we should expect a time of courtship when God showed himself to be a faithful and loving husband. The prophet Jeremiah reveals when and where that courtship took place: "as a bride you loved me and followed me through the desert, through a land not sown" (Jeremiah 2:2). What a way for God and his bride, Israel, to get to know one another! Six weeks traveling through the desert and experiencing the elation of leaving Egypt as free people, the dreadful fear (before) and overwhelming joy (after) of crossing the sea, the bitter complaining at Marah, the refreshing days at Elim, the gift of manna, water from the mountain of God, victory over the Amalekites, and at last arriving at Mount Sinai.

1. Using the chart on page 214, write down some of what God did for the Israelites during their "courtship" in the desert to demonstrate that he was a desirable husband who was worthy of their passionate love and devotion.

Text	How God "Courted" His Chosen People
Ex. 6:1–5	
Ex. 7:3–5	
Ex. 11:1–3; 12:31–36	
Ex. 14:5–9, 19–28	
Ex. 15:22–27	
Ex. 16:4, 11–15	
Ex. 17:5–6	
Ex. 17:10–16	

2. Now write down what the Israelites — the bride-to-be — did that would have made her desirable or undesirable to God.

Text	Ways Israel Was a Desirable or Undesirable Bride-to-Be
Ex. 4:29–31	
Ex. 6:6–9	
Ex. 12:50–51	
Ex. 14:10–12	
Ex. 14:31–15:18	

Text	Ways Israel Was a Desirable or Undesirable Bride-to-Be
Ex. 15:22 – 24	
Ex. 16:1 – 3, 8 – 9	
Ex. 16:13 – 20, 23 – 30	
Ex. 17:1 – 3, 7	

3. Imagine the anticipation of the bride and groom as they met together after their courtship in the desert.

    a. How do you think God felt as he watched his bride come across the desert and approach the foot of his mountain? (See Jeremiah 2:1 - 2; Isaiah 62:5.)

    b. How do you think Israel felt when God came to them at Mount Sinai? (See Exodus 19:16 - 19; Psalm 105:38 - 43; Isaiah 30:29.)

    c. In what ways do these images of God and his bride, Israel, help refresh your love and inspire delight in your relationship with God?

IN THE SINAI PENINSULA, MOUNTAINS LITERALLY RISE UP OUT OF THE DESERT FLOOR. IN PLACES SUCH AS THIS, WHICH IS WHERE THE TRADITIONAL MOUNT SINAI IS LOCATED, IT IS EASY TO SEE HOW GOD COULD SAY, "DON'T TOUCH THE MOUNTAIN!" IMAGINE WHAT AN IMPRESSIVE SIGHT IT WOULD BE FOR ISRAEL, GATHERED ON THE FLAT LAND IN FRONT OF THE MOUNTAINS, TO SEE GOD DESCENDING ON THE MOUNTAINTOP IN THE THUNDER, LIGHTNING, AND DEEP DARKNESS OF THE CLOUD OF HIS PRESENCE.

4. God is holy and makes no apologies for his holiness (Leviticus 19:1 – 2). Even though he is the one who makes his people holy, he also requires his people to become holy by obeying his commands (Leviticus 20:7 – 8; 22:31 – 32). So in a manner similar to a Jewish bride who prepares herself by taking a ritual bath (*mikveh*) the day before her wedding, God instructed Israel to make herself holy in preparation for meeting him at Mount Sinai.

   a. What instructions did God give to the Israelites to prepare for the wedding, and in what ways did these instructions communicate the need for holiness and purity before God? (See Exodus 19:9 – 15, 20 – 24.)

b. In the future, what makes the bride — the followers
of Jesus — ready for the wedding of the Lamb? (See
Hebrews 9:26 - 28; Revelation 19:7 - 8.)

DID YOU KNOW?
Becoming a Holy People

After the Israelites received the Torah and the "wedding" between God and
his people had taken place, the people declared, "Everything the Lᴏʀᴅ has
said we will do" (Exodus 24:3). So Moses wrote down everything the Lord
had revealed on Mount Sinai. Then he built an altar, set up twelve stone
pillars representing the twelve tribes of Israel, offered burnt offerings and
fellowship offerings of young bulls, sprinkled half the covenant blood on the
altar, and after reading the Book of the Covenant, sprinkled the other half of
the covenant blood on the people.

These actions symbolized that God had purified his people, sealed or rati-
fied their (marriage) covenant, and established fellowship (relationship) with
them. The Israelites knew they were forgiven, cleansed, and made holy by
God. Now they were a holy people who could live up to God's command to
be holy.

Much later Jesus, as mediator of the covenant, shed his blood for the remis-
sion of the sins of all humanity (Luke 22:20; Hebrews 9:27 – 28). He became
the substitute sacrifice for us, cleansing us and making us holy before God.

Reflection

God viewed the Israelites as his *segulah* — his treasured possession
(Exodus 19:5). But we also find another endearing word picture for
Israel in Deuteronomy 32:10: "he guarded him as the apple of his
eye." This Hebrew phrase for the "pupil" of the eye literally means
"the little man" of the eye. So God guarded his people as if they
were the apple — or pupil — of his eye.

To understand what this means, move your hand quickly (and safely!) toward the eye of someone you love very much. Notice how the eye, without the person's conscious thought, reflexively protects its pupil. This illustrates God's relationship with his people. He does not have to decide whether or not to protect his people; he loves them so much it is a natural action for him!

Next, look closely into the eyes of someone you love. Do you notice the "little person" in his/her eye? In a similar way, the image of his own people (and that includes your image) is the "little man" reflected in God's loving, twinkling eye.

> To what extent do you think God's image was reflected in Israel's eyes? And in yours?

> If you follow Jesus, do you truly believe that you are the "apple" of his eye? Why or why not?

> How much does it mean to you that he will never abandon you and instinctively acts in your best interest because he loves you so much?

God loved Israel with a passionate love that we cannot comprehend. He "courted" them by showing himself faithful and loving in the desert. At Mount Sinai he said, "I love you," and consecrated Israel to be his bride. Today, God still extends his love to his people; he is faithful and forgiving despite their failings, and he always desires an intimate relationship with them.

> How attractive and worthy of love is God to you today? Why?

If you follow Jesus, think of things he has done for you that make him like a husband you deeply desire and want to love intimately.

How easy or difficult is it for you to think of God being, in a sense, your husband who loves you and graciously receives the love that you demonstrate through obedience to him?

Although God is always generous and faithful in his love for us, what kinds of things do you do (or not do) that make you a less desirable bride? Ask him for his grace and strength as you seek to become more obedient and desirable to God.

Memorize

I call on you, O God, for you will answer me;
give ear to me and hear my prayer.
Show the wonder of your great love,
you who save by your right hand
those who take refuge in you from their foes.
Keep me as the apple of your eye;
hide me in the shadow of your wings.

Psalm 17:6 – 8

Day Two | God Places His Chuppah over Israel

The Very Words of God

On the morning of the third day there was thunder and lightning,
with a thick cloud over the mountain, and a very loud trumpet blast.
Everyone in the camp trembled. Then Moses led the people out of the

*camp to meet with God, and they stood at the foot of the mountain.
Mount Sinai was covered with smoke, because the L*ORD* descended on
it in fire. The smoke billowed up from it like smoke from a furnace, the
whole mountain trembled violently, and the sound of the trumpet grew
louder and louder.*

Exodus 19:16 – 19

Bible Discovery

The Protective Covering of God's Presence

In a traditional Jewish wedding, the bride and groom come together
under a *chuppah*, which literally means a "canopy" or "covering."
The *chuppah* symbolizes the protective covering God provides for
the couple as they begin their marriage. This beautiful picture is
rooted in the covering of God's presence that he provided when he
brought his bride, Israel, to Mount Sinai!

1. What covered Mount Sinai as evidence of God's presence
    when he met with Moses and Israel? (See Exodus 19:16 - 19;
    20:18 - 21; 24:15 - 18.)

    How had God prepared the Israelites to know what their
    meeting with him would be like? (See Exodus 19:9.)

    What had the Israelites done to prepare for their meeting
    with God? (See Exodus 19:10 - 17.)

Although the cloud of God's presence intimidated the people, were they truly frightened by it or were they confident that it represented God's presence and protection over them? How do you know this?

DID YOU KNOW?

On the appointed day, Israel stood "at the foot of the mountain" as God spoke to them (Exodus 19:17). This common translation communicates where the Hebrews were, but it does not capture the nuance of the Hebrew word that also implies being "under" or "beneath." So the Jewish interpretation sees Israel as not just standing at the base of the mountain but standing under God's great *chuppah* as represented by the cloud. The *chuppah* symbolized God's desire to choose the Hebrews out of all the nations and bring them into an intimate relationship with himself.

2. The *chuppah* has a special meaning in the context of marriage. What word picture is conveyed in Psalm 19:5 and Joel 2:15 – 16?

What sense of the significance and intimacy of the *chuppah's* covering do these passages give you?

DATA FILE
The Chuppah

The Hebrew *chuppah* is a canopy or covering traditionally used in Jewish weddings that represents the protective covering God provides for a couple as they begin their marriage. It consists of a cloth or sheet, or sometimes a *tallit* (prayer shawl), that is stretched over or supported by four poles and is open on all four sides.

A *chuppah* symbolizes the protective covering of God's presence as he brought his chosen people to Mount Sinai, which prophets later viewed as a wedding. It reminds or represents to the couple:

- That their relationship reflects God's relationship with his people
- The bridal chamber practices of the ancient Jewish people
- The home the couple will build together
- That Abraham's tent was always open for hospitality, so they also must show hospitality to their guests

3. A graphic image provided by the prophet Ezekiel helps us to comprehend the depth of God's love for his people and what it means to be brought under his canopy of love and protection. The story is set in the horrific practice of infant exposure as it was practiced in the ancient world. Unwanted newborns were simply left outdoors — sometimes in designated "dumps" — to die of exposure, to be eaten by animals, or to be salvaged by slave merchants. Using the language of infant exposure, Ezekiel describes the birth of God's people and how he brought them to himself. (See Ezekiel 16:1 – 14.)

   a. How deeply does God love his people, and how compassionately does he care for them?

   b. What commitment does God have to nurture life, beauty, purpose, and holiness in his people — regardless of the condition in which he finds them?

   c. What new understanding are you gaining about what it means to meet God under his *chuppah*, and to experience his intimate love and protection?

Reflection

The beautiful image of marriage and God's protective care that the *chuppah* represents as God met with his people — his bride — at Mount Sinai is still relevant today. According to Scripture, those of us who follow Christ are the bride of Christ. Therefore, God loves each of us and covers us with the canopy of his intimate, protective love.

In what way(s) has God demonstrated his "covering" of protection over you?

What do you think is God's *chuppah* — the symbol of his intimate love and protection — for you today?

Take some time to read Romans 8:28 – 39 and, as you read, think of the *chuppah,* God's covering over his people.

What was God willing to do to bring you under his *chuppah*?

Can anything defeat the protective covering of God's love for his people? Why or why not?

How closely will you cling to your God and experience the intimate love and care he offers to you under his *chuppah*?

POINT TO PONDER

In the culture of ancient Israel, premarital sex was almost nonexistent. The physical union of a couple was the "sacramental moment" of two people becoming one just as God had ordained when he created man and woman. Imagine the private, intimate, and sacred time a bride and groom spent in the bridal chamber (*chuppah*) consummating their marriage in the presence of God.

As time passed and the practice of bridal chambers changed, Jewish people were still married under a canopy. To be married under a *chuppah* was to recall the sacred moment of marriage as practiced among their ancient people. It was to retain the awe of that holy moment of physical and spiritual union that God created for a man and a woman through marriage.

In a sense, what occurred in the bridal chamber was instructive to the community. Certainly sexuality within marriage was practiced privately, but everyone knew what happened in the bridal chamber, which reinforced the fact that the sexual union was a sacred act to be practiced only within marriage. It is sad that our sex-saturated culture publicly flaunts sexuality and sexual behavior. Yet within God's community today, sexuality is dealt with in an almost secretive way — as if it does not exist. Perhaps a more open attitude about sexuality within marriage might prove instructive to children and young people and help to counteract the flagrant misuse of this God-given gift.

Day Three | God Prepares the Ketubah

The Very Words of God

> Then the LORD said to Moses ... "The Israelites are to observe the
> Sabbath, celebrating it for the generations to come as a lasting
> covenant. It will be a sign between me and the Israelites forever, for in
> six days the LORD made the heavens and the earth, and on the seventh
> day he abstained from work and rested." When the LORD finished
> speaking to Moses on Mount Sinai, he gave him the two tablets of the
> Testimony, the tablets of stone inscribed by the finger of God.
>
> *Exodus 31:12, 16 – 18*

Bible Discovery

Establishing an Intimate Relationship with God

During ancient times, covenants formally defined many kinds of relationships, including the marriage relationship. Covenants were documented carefully to spell out the mutually agreed upon responsibilities and commitments of the parties involved. Even today, traditional Jewish weddings echo this ancient practice in the reading of a *ketubah* (Hebrew for "marriage contract") during the ceremony when the bride is under the *chuppah*. Much like vows in a Christian wedding, the *ketubah* spells out the commitments the bride and groom make to each other.

Although the Bible records no examples of a *ketubah*, examples from late biblical times have been found. No one would argue that the Ten Commandments were a formal *ketubah*, but the Ten Commandments could be viewed in this light. The Bible describes Israel as God's bride (Jeremiah 2:2), so in keeping with the marriage metaphor, the Ten Commandments could be viewed as a *ketubah*.

1. At the heart of Israel's relationship with the Lord was a deep and intimate exchange of love, like that found between a husband and wife.

   a. What did God do for his people that expressed a deep love for them? (See Exodus 19:3–6; Deuteronomy 7:6–9, 12.)

   b. What did God ask the Hebrews to do for him, and what would such actions express to him? (See Deuteronomy 4:5–14; 6:4–9, 20–25; 10:12–15.)

2. The Ten Commandments are God's ten vows or guidelines for a good relationship — that is, a good "marriage" — like the one he desired to have with his ancient people. Because

he loved his people, God gave them the Ten Commandments to show them how to love him. Read Exodus 20:1 – 17 aloud and read slowly.

a.　On which act did God base his commands for his people? (See Exodus 20:2.)

b.　For what kind of relationship did God create these commands? (See Jeremiah 2:2; Isaiah 54:5; 62:5.)

c.　Now consider how the Ten Commandments, if viewed as the *ketubah* for the mutual relationship between God and his people, would have shaped their relationship. The first four commandments, which focus on expressing the love between God and his people, have been restated in marital language.

"You shall have no other gods." — "You shall have no husbands or lovers other than me."

Which phrases did God use to describe Israel's later idolatry, and how does this strengthen the idea that God wanted Israel to view the Torah as a marriage covenant? (See 1 Chronicles 5:23 – 25; Jeremiah 3:6 – 14; 5:7 – 11.)

"You shall not make idols or images nor worship them." — "You shall not even have pictures or replicas of other lovers."

How did God view lusting after idols or images, and what impact does such wrongdoing still have on marriages today? (See Ezekiel 6:1 – 10.)

"Do not use my name in vain." — "You now bear my name: honor it and use it wisely."

In the ancient world, a person and his/her name were considered as one and the same, so to dishonor someone's name was to dishonor the person. Why is it significant that God placed his name on the Israelites, and what does it reveal about their relationship to God and their mission in the world? (See Numbers 6:22 – 27; 2 Chronicles 7:14, Isaiah 43:4 – 7.)

"Keep the Sabbath day holy [set apart]" — "I want you to set aside time to love me."

In the beginning, what did God establish for the seventh day (Genesis 2:1 – 3), and what does Exodus 31:12 – 17 reveal about the Sabbath's role in his relationship with Israel?

NOTE: Keeping the Sabbath set apart for God is essential to honoring him as sovereign Creator, but it is also necessary for God's people to set aside time from their other responsibilities in order to build and to enjoy their intimate relationship with him. Intimate relationships do not thrive when time is not set aside to nurture them.

d. The next six commandments have to do with the relationships of God's people to one another. In what ways do these commandments strengthen community, bring honor to God, and reveal who he is to the world? (See Exodus 20:12 – 17.)

Honor your father and mother.

Do not murder.

Do not commit adultery.

Do not steal.

Do not bear false witness.

Do not covet.

DATA FILE

In the Hebrew Bible, the Ten Commandments are called the "ten words" (Exodus 34:28, Deuteronomy 4:13; 10:4). This description, and the fact that the commandments are bluntly brief, have led scholars to suggest that the commandments originally were ten Hebrew words, which would have made them easy to remember and powerful in their effect. The words were probably on the order of "No-adultery," "No-steal," "No-murder," "No-images," "No-other gods," and so on. This would have been easier to do in Hebrew than in English. One can just imagine the Israelites reciting them as they touched their ten fingers.

The exact numbering of the commandments has been argued for millennia. The Jewish tradition and various Christian traditions, although having exactly

continued on next page . . .

the same content, divide the content differently to make ten. The Jewish numbering is likely the one that people of biblical times would have known. The numbering used in this session is the Protestant numbering.

Division of the Ten Commandments by Faith Tradition				
Commandment	Protestant	Roman Catholic	Orthodox	Jewish
I am the Lord your God	Preface	1	1	1
You shall have no other gods before me	1			2
You shall not make for yourself an idol	2		2	
You shall not make wrongful use of the name of your God	3	2	3	3
Remember the Sabbath and keep it holy	4	3	4	4
Honor your father and mother	5	4	5	5
You shall not kill	6	5	6	6
You shall not commit adultery	7	6	7	7
You shall not steal	8	7	8	8
You shall not bear false witness against your neighbor	9	8	9	9
You shall not covet your neighbor's wife	10	9	10	10
You shall not covet anything that belongs to your neighbor		10		

DATA FILE
The Covenant Document

God created human beings with the deep need to be in relationship with him. After Adam and Eve sinned, breaking the friendship between God and his creation, he developed a plan that would restore his relationship with them. The relationship between God and his chosen people, Israel, was central to that plan, so in order to help the Israelites understand the depth of his love and commitment, God sealed their relationship with a marriage covenant.

In the ancient Near East, covenants were a familiar form of cultural agreements. The fundamental difference between covenants and other agreements was the *relationship* established between the covenant makers. Each party made specific promises and expected certain benefits (and penalties, if the promises were broken) according to the terms of the covenant. Obligations of a covenant relationship were based more on the friendship established by the covenant than on the legalities.

Although today's Bible translations refer to people "making" a covenant, the Hebrews used the term "cutting" a covenant. The cutting, symbolized by the slaughter of animals (Exodus 24:5, 8), indicated that each person in the covenant promised to give his or her life in order to keep its terms. Covenants were made before witnesses — sometimes things (Genesis 31:51 – 52), sometimes God (Genesis 31:53). Symbols were often used to remind the parties of their covenants (Genesis 9:12 – 16; 31:43 – 48).

Ancient covenant documents, such as those Moses carried, often were made of stone or baked clay. (Typically stone was used only for permanent inscriptions, such as royal or national inscriptions.) Usually these tablets were four to six inches wide, eight to twelve inches tall, and inscribed on both sides. The much larger tablets with curved tops first appeared about a millennium ago, more than two thousand years after God gave his covenant to Moses.

Due to the complex relationships often documented in a covenant, they usually were quite long. So a summary document representing the total relationship between the parties was also provided. If the Torah is God's covenant with Israel, the Ten Commandments inscribed on stone tablets is

continued on next page . . .

the summary document. Normally, each party kept a copy of this document in a sacred place. When God gave both tablets to Moses, he was making a profound statement. Trusting Moses with his copy indicated that God's sacred place was the same as Israel's: the ark of the covenant in the Holy of Holies in the tabernacle.

Reflection

God used the Torah, and in summary the Ten Commandments, to express his eternal love for his people, to define his relationship with them, and to show them how to love him and maintain an intimate relationship with him. To read God's covenant is to discover not only God's will for human society but how deeply he loves the people he created. Through the covenant relationship, he was willing to prove his devotion by offering his life to keep the covenant — even if it failed because of the human beings with whom he was in relationship. And it did fail. But in Christ God fulfilled his promise to give his own life to seal the covenant he made with the Israelites. For this reason, Jesus could say, "Do not think that I have come to abolish the Law or the Prophets; I have not come to abolish them but to fulfill them" (Matthew 5:17).

What an indescribable gift God gave to Israel through his covenant with them! Did you know that God is still making a covenant with his people? Unlike the former covenant written on tablets of stone, where is God's covenant being written today? (See Jeremiah 31:31 – 34; Proverbs 7:1 – 3; 2 Corinthians 3:1 – 3; Hebrews 10:15 – 16.)

Where, then, is the sacred place where God, by his Spirit, meets with his people?

What is the covenant between you and God that is written on your heart?

Is the relationship of your covenant with God as intimate as that between a loving husband and wife?

In what ways does the degree of intimacy in your relationship with God affect the passion, commitment, and love you express to him?

A covenant relationship in marriage is a powerful expression of love. In what ways has what you have learned about God's covenant with his people influenced:

your appreciation of his love for you?

your attitude toward obeying him — in everything?

your commitment to nurture your relationship with him by taking time out on the Sabbath?

Memorize

Are we beginning to commend ourselves again? Or do we need, like some people, letters of recommendation to you or from you? You yourselves are our letter, written on our hearts, known and read by everybody. You show that you are a letter from Christ, the result of our ministry, written not with ink but with the Spirit of the living God, not on tablets of stone but on tablets of human hearts.

2 Corinthians 3:1 – 3

DATA FILE
Parts of a Covenant

In general, ancient Near Eastern covenants had five sections:

The Preamble identified the parties of the covenant. In the Torah, God established the identities of the parties in the creation story. He was the Creator, Israel his creation. In the Ten Commandments, he said simply, "I am the LORD your God" (Exodus 20:2).

The Historical Prologue recited the history leading to the cutting of the covenant to prove the right of the superior party to make it. The Torah details the stories of the fall, Noah, Abraham, and the exodus as the basis for God's covenant with Moses. In the Ten Commandments, the summary is simply "… who brought you out of Egypt, out of the land of slavery" (Exodus 20:2).

Requirements (Commandments). In the Torah, God placed 613 requirements on the Israelites and even more obligations on himself. The Ten Commandments summarized ten (Exodus 20:3 – 17), and scholars have noted that Jesus reduced his summary to just two (Matthew 22:37 – 40).

Blessings and Curses included the rewards for keeping the covenant and penalties for breaking it. See Moses' summary in Deuteronomy 28, and in the Ten Commandments.

The Summary Document briefly summarized the covenant and was kept in each party's sacred place.

Day Four | The Bride Has an Affair!

The Very Words of God

> *When the people saw that Moses was so long in coming down from the mountain, they gathered around Aaron and said, "Come, make us gods who will go before us. As for this fellow Moses who brought us up out of Egypt, we don't know what has happened to him." ... So all the people took off their earrings and brought them to Aaron. He took what they handed him and made it into an idol cast in the shape of a calf, fashioning it with a tool. Then they said, "These are your gods, O Israel, who brought you up out of Egypt."*
>
> *Exodus 32:1, 3 – 4*

Bible Discovery

God Continues to Love His Unfaithful Bride

Picture in your mind thousands of Israelites — the bride of God — camped near Mount Sinai. They had experienced God's power when he delivered them from Egypt and his loving care as their provider and protector in the wilderness. When God came down to them, fire, smoke, thunder, and the trembling of the earth beneath their feet filled their senses. Their God had come to speak with them! They promised to obey him, but while Moses was on the mountain with God, they seem to have forgotten the covenant they had just made with their loving, faithful God. They turned their affection toward a golden calf! Why would they do this, and how would God respond?

1. What kind of love did God have for his people, and what kind of relationship was he establishing with them at Mount Sinai? (See Exodus 19:3 – 6; Ezekiel 16:8.)

2. Israel made some specific promises in order to express their love for God and protect the sanctity of their ongoing relationship with him, but quickly reneged when put to the test. Use the chart on page 236 to answer questions a, b, and c.

What Israel Agreed Not to Do	What Israel Did	What God Observed

a. Which specific acts had the Israelites agreed not to do? (See Exodus 20:3 – 6, 23.)

b. While Moses was in the presence of God getting the tablets — the *ketubah*, the sacred and exclusive relationship between God and Israel — the people camped at the bottom of the mountain were getting restless. What does it seem the Israelites and Aaron believed had happened to Moses, and what did they do about it? (See Exodus 24:17 – 18; 32:1 – 6.)

c. What did God say Israel had done, and how did he respond? (See Exodus 32:7 – 14.)

d. What do you think was in the Israelites' hearts and minds that permitted them to make such a solemn and exclusive relational agreement with God and then so quickly cast it aside? What warning might this serve to you in your relationship with God?

FOR GREATER UNDERSTANDING
Why a Golden Calf?

It is not surprising that Aaron, who somehow thought that Moses would not return and that God could be worshiped in ways other than those he had specified, chose the form of a calf to represent the god(s) the Israelites would follow. Signifying strength, fertility, power, and leadership, the symbol of a cow or bull was a common representation of deity (not the deity itself), particularly that of Apis and Hathor in the Egyptian culture. Based on other examples of calf idols, the one Aaron made may have been only a foot tall and could have served as the pedestal on which the god was believed to stand—whether it was the God of the Bible or one of the gods of Egypt.

Which Egyptian god might the golden calf have represented to the Israelites? Some scholars think they were influenced more by the worship of Hathor—the supposed wife of Horus and daughter of Re—than by worship of the god Apis, whom worshipers believed was present in the sacred bull image. Hathor was Egypt's greatest and most enduring goddess. She was associated with love and sexuality, so the revelry or orgy that followed the

THIS CUT STONE FOUND IN THE TEMPLE OF HATHOR AT SERABIT AL KHADIM IN THE SINAI DESERT IS A TYPICAL PORTRAYAL OF THE BULL ASSOCIATED WITH EGYPTIAN GODS SUCH AS HATHOR.

continued on next page . . .

sacrifice to the calf idol fits the practices of the Hathor cult (Exodus 32:6). Hathor also was believed to be the goddess of foreign lands, which may have influenced the Israelites who were traveling to the Promised Land.

There's another reason to think that the golden calf may have been a representation of Hathor. Although no one knows the exact location of Mount Sinai where Aaron made the golden calf, there is an ancient Egyptian mining settlement about two days' walk from the traditional Mount Sinai. In that settlement, there is a temple to Hathor, who was also the goddess of desert mining! Egyptian turquoise miners originally built the temple in about 1800 BC, and the traditional Mount Sinai can be seen from the plateau on which the temple is built.

It is unclear whether the Israelites actually passed by this temple. However, if they did it would make sense for them to believe that they were in the territory of Hathor's rule (Egypt's gods are local), and thus choose to make the calf idol for that reason. No matter which details of location or reasoning come into play, this story illustrates how difficult it was for the Israelites to escape Egypt and its pagan worldview. Their conduct after sacrificing to the golden calf supports the idea that they were still greatly influenced by their Egyptian past.

THIS REMOTE TEMPLE OF THE EGYPTIAN GODDESS HATHOR OVERLOOKS THE WILDERNESS OF SIN IN THE SINAI PENINSULA. BUILT IN ABOUT 1800 BC, IT IS ABOUT TWO DAYS' WALK FROM THE TRADITIONAL MOUNT SINAI.

3. When Moses saw the calf and the behavior of the Israelites, what was his response, and why was it significant in light of what Israel had just done to their covenant with God? (See Exodus 32:19 – 30.)

NOTE: When a covenant was broken in the ancient Near East, the offended party would publicly break the tablets on which the covenant was written as a symbol of what had happened. So when Moses broke the tablets, he was expressing more than his own righteous anger about the Israelites breaking their covenant with God.

What additional action did Moses take against the Israelites, and what was his motivation?

DID YOU KNOW?

The Hebrew word describing what happened at the festival "to the LORD" (Exodus 32:5 – 6) that took place in front of the golden calf can have strong sexual overtones that are similar to the English word "orgy." Celebrations of the Egyptian gods Apis and Hathor typically included having sexual relations. Furthermore, because a woman's jewelry, particularly earrings, were symbols of marriage, it is possible that the Israelite women may have contributed their "wedding bands" to make the calf! What an irony that Israel, God's bride, was unfaithful to him by disobeying his commands and worshiping an idol, and also by celebrating their disobedience by having sexual relations!

4. What action did Moses take before God in response to what Israel had done? (See Exodus 32:11 – 14, 30 – 35; 33:12 – 17.)

What was his motivation, and what was God's response?

What do you see in Moses that illustrates zeal for the Lord, a passion for righteousness, and a compassionate and forgiving heart that is willing to bear the penalty for someone else's sin? In what ways does this remind you of a "prophet" whom God promised would come later?

POINT TO PONDER
God's Stiff-Necked People

In Exodus 34:8 – 9, Moses seems to have used Israel's attitude of being stiff necked, which so often got them into trouble with God, as an argument for why God should go with them to the Promised Land. Jewish sages have wondered why Moses used this condition, which brought God's anger against Israel, as his argument for why God should go with them. Perhaps it is because their greatest weakness — willful, stiff-necked obstinateness — would become a great strength when transformed into faithfulness. Throughout history, Israel vacillated between these two extremes — obstinate resistance or obstinate faithfulness. Sometimes, by refusing to violate their covenant relationship with God, they faced humiliation, persecution, torture, and even died by the thousands. That stubbornness was a great virtue.[1]

Reflection

How quickly Israel reverted to idol worship — even during the "wedding" as God prepared the Ten Commandments! Although God was angry, he did not abandon his bride despite her blatant unfaithfulness.

> Why do you think it was so hard for the Israelites to be faithful to God, even after he rescued them from slavery, brought them to Sinai, and made a covenant with them as if they were his bride?

Like Israel, we can find ourselves "going back to Egypt" in thoughts, words, and actions. Yet God stands ready to forgive us and bring us back into right relationship with him, just as he did with Israel. Take a moment to reflect on the ways you have been unfaithful to God and betrayed your relationship with him.

> What have you said or done that God would view as adultery?

> What pain has your betrayal of your relationship with God caused him?

What insights has the "golden calf" incident given you regarding the forgiving, holy, and righteous character of God?

When you consider that the covenant between God and his people included building the tabernacle where he would come and live with them (Exodus 25:8 – 9), how significant is it that God would forgive Israel for being unfaithful and once again instruct Moses in how to build the tabernacle (Exodus 35 – 39)?

What does God's willingness to try again to build a place to live with his people say to you about the depth of his love and his commitment to you?

Besides Moses, who else in Scripture was willing to take on himself God's anger at the sins of his people?

What appreciation for his sacrifice have you gained as a result of this study?

FOR GREATER UNDERSTANDING
The Forgiving Heart of God

The story of Hosea parallels how God felt when Israel — his bride — betrayed her relationship and committed spiritual adultery by pursuing other gods. The heartache and the love revealed in Hosea's story helps us see the impact of our unfaithfulness on the heart of God. Hosea married Gomer, an adulterous woman, because God wanted their relationship to be an example of his relationship with his adulterous bride, Israel (Hosea 1 – 3). Hosea's sensitive description of his relationship suggests that he loved Gomer deeply, but she left him and took a series of lovers. Hosea loved her anyway, and in his grief he discovered the intensity of God's love for Israel.

God, as we know, had rescued his bride, Israel, from slavery. He had courted her in the barren desert (Hosea 2:14) and was betrothed to her at Mount Sinai. But immediately his bride chose another lover — the golden calf — an abomination that the prophets compared to adultery. Yet God, despite his anger and hurt, did not give up on his beloved. After he disciplined her (2:1 – 13), he remained faithful to Israel, seeking out his people even when they were completely unfaithful to him.

The Jewish people have recognized Hosea 2:19 – 20 as a pure expression of the love God desires in the relationship between himself and his bride. So they read this text on the Sabbath before *Shavuoth*, the date they believe the Torah was given on Mount Sinai. In so doing, they affirm that God was not simply displaying his power and lordship over Israel when he gave the Torah to his people, but was declaring his passionate love for them. This declaration of love is also why Jewish men recite these verses every weekday morning before praying, as a way of renewing their wedding vows.

Day Five | Celebrate the Covenant

The Very Words of God

> *I will betroth you to me forever;*
> > *I will betroth you in righteousness and justice,*
> > *in love and compassion.*
> *I will betroth you in faithfulness,*
> > *and you will acknowledge the Lord.*

Hosea 2:19 – 20

Bible Discovery

Obedience: The Language of Love

God deeply loved Israel and delivered his people from bondage in order to bring them into a personal and intimate relationship with himself — their "husband" and King. Because they already *were* his people and God had established a relationship of love with them, God expected the Israelites to show their true love for him through obedience as required by the terms of their covenant. Obedience was the "love language" by which God wanted his people — his bride — to express their love toward him.

1. God made a covenant with Israel that is summarized in the Ten Commandments (Exodus 20:1 - 17). That summary expresses both his commitment to bring his people (his bride) to himself and the expressions of love toward him that would keep his people in a right relationship with him.

   a. On what basis did God give Israel the opportunity to have a covenant relationship of love with him? (See Deuteronomy 7:6 - 8; 10:14 - 15.)

   b. How were the Israelites to demonstrate their love for God because he had brought them to himself like a bride? (See Exodus 20:6; Deuteronomy 6:4 - 8; 7:9; 10:12 - 13; 11:1; 30:16.)

   c. Considering all that you have learned about God making his covenant with Israel at Mount Sinai and summarizing the terms of that covenant in the Ten Commandments, what new understanding do you have regarding obedience as the love language of Israel's relationship with God?

2. Who else in the Bible is described as the bride of God? (See John 3:22 – 30; 2 Corinthians 11:2; Ephesians 5:22 – 33; Revelation 19:5 – 8.)

On what basis does God give people today the opportunity to become one of his own — his bride? (See John 3:16; Ephesians 2:4 – 10; 2 Timothy 1:8 – 10.)

How are God's people today to demonstrate their love for God because he has brought them to himself? (See Matthew 7:21; Luke 6:46 – 49; John 14:15, 23 – 24; 1 John 2:1 – 6; 5:3; 2 John 6.)

Do you think obedience is still the language of love God wants his people to use in relationship with him? Why or why not?

FOR GREATER UNDERSTANDING
Saved by Grace

Much as Jewish tradition emphasizes the mercy of God toward his people, Christian tradition emphasizes the saving grace of Jesus. Salvation by grace is clearly the Bible's teaching. Some Christians, however, may overlook the fact that this is true in the Hebrew text as well as the Christian text.

Deuteronomy 7:6–8 makes it clear that God redeemed the Hebrews from Egypt and from their sin because of his love for them, not because they did anything to earn or deserve his deliverance. Just as he still does today, God pursued his people and delivered them from bondage in order to bring them into an intimate relationship with him as their husband and King. God requires obedience not to make people his own, but because they *are* his people. So obedience to God doesn't carry the burden of earning one's relationship with God. Rather, it is our joyful response to the faithful love of God who establishes the relationship.

3. What did God tell Moses would be the sign of Israel's covenant relationship with God? (See Exodus 31:12 – 17; Ezekiel 20:10 – 20.)

   How important was this sign to God, and what did it celebrate?

   How would observing this sign demonstrate Israel's commitment to be a faithful bride to God?

THINK ABOUT IT

The Sabbath was the sign of the covenant relationship between God and Israel. Keeping the Sabbath was a weekly celebration of the love and commitment of that relationship. During the other six days of the week, Israel was busy carrying out their responsibilities in obedience (love) to God. The Sabbath, however, was time set aside from work so that God and Israel — his bride — could spend time together to develop an intimate, loving relationship.

Is keeping the Sabbath — the sign of the covenant relationship between God and his bride — still important for followers of Jesus today? Is keeping the Sabbath set apart still central to honoring God and submitting to his plan for his creation? Is keeping the Sabbath and celebrating their relationship to God still important for the bride of Christ?

4. Shortly before he died, Moses summarized the total commitment to loving the Lord. (See Deuteronomy 6:4 – 9; 11:13 – 21.)

  a. To what extent do Moses' words express your commitment to loving God in all of life?

  b. Is your love for God such that you are eager to express it by obeying his commands in every way possible? If not, why not?

DATA FILE
What Is the Shema?

The *shema* has been a central statement of faith for Jewish people since ancient times. Spoken by Moses shortly before he died, this passage (Deuteronomy 6:4–9; 11:13–21) summarized the total commitment God expected from his people because God brought them to himself at Sinai. Jewish people have recited the *shema* every morning and evening since before Jesus was born in order to have these words in mind when they get up and lie down.

The passage is named *shema* after its first Hebrew word that means "hear"—to listen or obey. It is like a father saying to a child, "You did not *listen* to me." He does not mean the child did not hear the words. Rather, he is saying, "You did not do what I asked."

Jewish people have long understood that loving God is not just an emotional feeling or statement of love or commitment, any more than the love between a man and woman in marriage is simply the statement of their love at a wedding. To love God requires the total commitment of one's heart, soul, and strength. This is the way in which one accepts the kingship of God and expresses devotion in accepting the responsibility of keeping God's commandments. It is the way to "take the yoke of the kingdom of heaven." It is the public witness to God and community that a person accepts the command to fulfill the obligations of the covenant God made with his people.

Saying *shema* is a daily commitment to love God by keeping his commandments. If the Torah is, among other things, an expression of God's "marriage" relationship to his people, the *shema* gives voice to each person repeating his/her commitment to that relationship. It might be compared to a husband or wife repeating their marriage vows every day after the wedding. The *shema* is the first passage of Scripture a child is taught. Jesus and his disciples likely recited the *shema* as the first and last act of every day. The *shema* was, and is, the greatest commandment.

Reflection

God gave Israel the Ten Commandments as a way of expressing his passionate love for them, and their obedience expressed their love for him. Today, followers of Jesus have the same mission to the world that the Israelites had: to display God not just by what we say, but by who we are as a result of our faithful obedience to his commands. How can we reflect God's holiness, his desire for justice, his love for the broken, the hurting, the outsider ... if we fail to love him with all our heart, soul, and strength?

If you are a follower of Jesus, how might viewing your obedience to his commands as your "love language" to your spiritual husband encourage you to eagerly and passionately obey him?

What do you believe the walk of a person who loves God should look like?

How closely does your walk resemble that of a person who loves God passionately?

What specific steps will you take to obey God's commands more fully, thus demonstrating the depth of your love for him?

To what extent is it a serious problem that the walk of followers of Jesus is sometimes not much different from that of people who do not yet know him?

How central do you think a deep commitment to obediently following God should be to the Christian community?

Why is the *shema* just as important for God's people today to remember (and keep) as it was for God's people during ancient times?

How important is it to you, and how can you keep it before you?

Memorize

Hear, O Israel: The Lord our God, the Lord is one. Love the Lord your God with all your heart and with all your soul and with all your strength.

Deuteronomy 6:4 – 5

DATA FILE
Sew Tassels on the Corners of Your Garments

In the ancient culture in which God gave this command, people decorated their garments in ways that showed societal identity and status. An outer robe's hem and tassels were particularly important. In fact, the corner of the hem would be pressed into clay to leave a person's official seal.

Moses told Israel that tassels sewn onto the hem were a constant visual reminder of the commandments God gave at Mount Sinai. By wearing tassels, God's people wore what appeared to be the robe of royalty that helped to remind them that they were God's holy, chosen people. Wearing a rare and expensive blue or purple thread in the tassel — the color of the priests' robes — reminded the Israelites that God chose them out of all nations and peoples to be a kingdom of priests who would display their God to the world.[2] Perhaps the tassels also reminded them to obey God completely so that by wearing the robe they would not be hypocrites.

Through their unusual dress, the Israelites were making a public declaration that they belonged to the Most High God. If they compromised their identity — their witness — by failing to obey God's commands, they would present a flawed picture of God. That would mislead other nations, which would anger God because he hates sin and wants all people to experience him and follow his ways.

Many followers of Jesus today are Gentiles, who have not been commanded to wear tassels. But those who have been redeemed in Jesus are also a royal priesthood and holy nation whose mission is to witness to the world of the amazing, redeeming love of God (1 Peter 2:9, 12). Like the ancient Israelites, we are not simply to bear witness but to be a witness. Our lives are to communicate that the Lord is God in whom is found genuine hope and life. Our obedience is our response to God's act of choosing us; it is our way of faithfully carrying out the mission he has given us.

THE WHISPER OF GOD: MOSES AND ELIJAH ON THE MOUNTAIN OF GOD

Exodus 32 – 34; 1 Kings 19:1 – 18

After crossing the Red Sea and the vast deserts of the Sinai Peninsula, the Israelites arrived at the mountain of God. For them, it was a completely new experience, but Moses had been to God's mountain before — when God spoke to him from the burning bush. At that time, God told Moses that the proof of his presence would be that the Israelites would come to worship him at that same mountain. Just as he had promised, God revealed his presence to the Israelites at Mount Sinai and met with Moses again.

Moses is not the only great Bible figure who met God on Mount Sinai, however. Hundreds of years later, Elijah met God there too. Although they ministered in different places and during different times in Israel's history, both Moses and Elijah played prominent roles in shepherding the flock of God's people. Some of their experiences with God are remarkably similar.

For example, both Moses and Elijah were called prophets who served God passionately as they fulfilled their respective roles in his plan for redeeming the world. Both confronted God's people for chasing after pagan gods and led his people back to faithfulness. They both went to the same mountain (perhaps even the same cave?) where God showed himself to these faithful men who loved and lived the biblical text. Both men boldly declared their desires to God, who rewarded them by allowing them to experience him in extraordinarily intimate ways. There, one-on-one with God on his holy mountain, but mercifully sheltered from full exposure to his mighty presence, they witnessed his awesome power. More importantly, they experienced his gentleness, mercy, and love — and that transformed their lives. Even their death experiences shared a strange, holy quality that is unlike that of any other Bible characters.

The story and testimony of these great men of God did not come to an end, even in death. In a sense they "returned" — together — on another mountain, in another place, at another time, to herald a third great prophetic figure of the Bible whose life in some ways echoed their own. In an event known by Christians as the transfiguration, Jesus was mysteriously transformed by divine power in the company of Moses and Elijah, sending a powerful message that Jesus was indeed the Son of God. This central story in the Christian text is deeply rooted in the stories of Moses and Elijah and was anticipated in the Jewish traditions of the time.

The gentleness, mercy, and love that Jesus demonstrated throughout his earthly life reaffirmed the character of God — the same aspects of his character that he revealed to Moses and Elijah on Mount Sinai. As Moses and Elijah — and so many people since ancient times — discovered, God's awesome power makes an impact, but God's gentleness, mercy, and love are what truly transforms people. Jesus, the Son of God, whose life echoed the intimate whisper heard by Moses and Elijah, ultimately set the example we should follow as we step into our role in fulfilling God's plan for redeeming the world.

So come, explore the lives of Moses and Elijah as they came to the mountain of God. Through them we will not only recognize the Creator of the universe as he revealed himself to and through them, but we will better understand Jesus the Messiah and the ways by which he revealed the very nature of God through his own ministry and person.

Opening Thoughts (4 minutes)

The Very Words of God

> *The LORD said, "Go out and stand on the mountain in the presence of the LORD, for the LORD is about to pass by." Then a great and powerful wind tore the mountains apart and shattered the rocks before the LORD, but the LORD was not in the wind. After the wind there was an earthquake, but the LORD was not in the earthquake. After the earthquake came a fire, but the LORD was not in the fire. And after the fire came a gentle whisper.*
>
> *1 Kings 19:11 – 12*

Think About It

When we reflect on who God is and what he is like, one aspect or another of his character usually stands out to us as being the most memorable or impressive. Some of us may see God as being loving or forgiving while others may see him as being angry or judgmental.

When you think about who God is, which personal characteristics come to mind? What do you imagine it might be like to actually meet God face to face?

DVD Notes (21 minutes)

Moses encounters God on his mountain

Called by name—twice

Elijah in the shade of a broom tree

Moses and Elijah hear the whisper of God

DVD Discussion (8 minutes)

1. Think of the images of the Sinai desert — the steep, rocky mountains; the lack of water and vegetation; the scorching heat of the sun reflected from great expanses of rock and sand.

   a. What do you think it would be like to be a shepherd in that wilderness?

b. Which character qualities might a person develop in the process of leading sheep to safe water and food there?

2. On the map of Lower Egypt and the Sinai Peninsula, locate Jebel Katarina and Jebel Musa in the mountains of southern Sinai. Although neither of these peaks is necessarily the actual mountain where Moses and Elijah met God, they represent what that mountain would have been like.

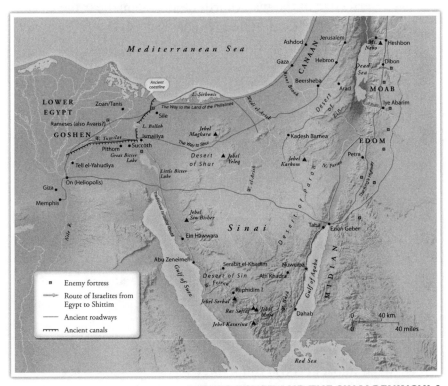

LOWER EGYPT AND THE SINAI PENINSULA

Consider too that most of the land east of the Nile River (with the exception of the land of Canaan from the coast to the mountains of Judea where Beersheba, Hebron, and Jerusalem are located) is desert. So no matter on which mountain in the desert Moses and Elijah met God, they were in the midst of a vast, barren wilderness.

a. Would talking with God be important enough to you to begin a long journey into that wilderness with no apparent preparation? Why or why not?

b. When you consider that Mount Carmel, where Elijah confronted the prophets of Baal, is just beyond the northern edge of the map (north of Jerusalem, near the coast), it is no wonder it took him forty days to reach the mountain of God.

c. About how many miles is it from the Nile Delta or Beersheba to the mountains of southern Sinai?

3. What thoughts did the scenes of the cold spring high up on the mountain bring to mind regarding God's faithful provision, in even the most barren, hostile places?

4. What impact do you think the whisper of God's voice had on Moses and Elijah as they continued serving God and interacting with his people in order to fulfill the mission he had given to them?

To what extent do you think God's people today hear the whisper of his voice?

What difference do you think his voice makes in the life and ministry of those who serve him?

5. Which personal qualities and characteristics do you think made Moses and Elijah such great men of God?

To what extent does the community of God's people today value and nurture these qualities and characteristics?

Small Group Bible Discovery and Discussion (20 minutes)

What It Means to Be a Servant of God

The life story of Moses shows God's purposeful preparation of the man who would be "as God to Pharaoh" and bring God's people out of bondage in Egypt. Moses would be God's partner in shaping God's people into his "treasured possession," a kingdom of priests and a holy nation (Exodus 19:5 – 6). He would be God's instrument in providing the Torah, the document of God's covenant with his people. And he would become the paradigm for all godly prophets to follow. What can we learn about Moses' life that will give us insight into what shaped him to become a servant of God?

1. Consider the cultural, spiritual, and familial influences that shaped Moses as a child and as an adult. As you read the following passages, note as many examples of these shaping influences as you can.

    a. *Exodus 1:6 - 22.* Into what kind of social environment was Moses born? What kinds of conflicts dominated everyday life? How might those conflicts have shaped him?

    b. *Exodus 2:1 - 10.* What did Moses' birth family value, and what were they motivated to risk in order to live by those values? What did Pharaoh's daughter evidently value? How might these values have shaped Moses?

    c. *Acts 7:20 - 28.* What kind of an education did Moses receive, and how might it have influenced his understanding of his role in life?

    d. In what ways did these influences prepare Moses to do God's work?

THINK ABOUT IT
A Life in God's Hands

Even during such dark times for the Hebrew people as the days of brutal enslavement by the Egyptians, God was at work in the lives and hearts of his people. Although some of his chosen people turned away from him to worship Egyptian gods, others remained faithful to the God of their ancestors. Consider, for example, Moses' parents and grandparents. Moses' mother was named Jochebed, which in Hebrew means "praise the Lord." His father was named Amram, which means "exalted nation or people." What kind of faith would cause slaves to give their children names that expressed such bold optimism and hope?

What kind of parents would defy the Pharaoh in order to preserve the life of their newborn son? And when hiding Moses at home was no longer possible, could Jochebed have deliberately chosen a hiding place where he was likely to be found? The Nile River is frequently crocodile infested, and a princess would not bathe in public, so is it possible that Moses' basket was hidden in the reeds of a channel close to the palace? Was Moses' sister watching over him because they expected someone to find him? Or, was it purely God's providence? Either way, do you see God's hand at work?

What a bold move Moses' sister, Miriam, made when she asked the princess if she could find a nurse for the child — especially since the nurse would be the child's own mother! In the ancient world, a wet nurse (a nursing woman chosen to help suckle the baby) was quite common. Wet nurses also acted as tutors and guardians for the children during the first few years of life. Certainly Jochebed took every opportunity to nurture Moses' mind and character, and teach him the traditions of his ancestors.

Think about the irony of an Egyptian princess finding Moses. Pharaoh's daughter defied his command in order to save the very child God would use to break the power of the dynasty of which she was a part and to free the Hebrew slaves. She gave him the best education and training that Egypt could offer, and she named him Moses, which is *moshe* in Hebrew and

continued on next page . . .

means "draw or pull out." Without even knowing it, she gave Moses his destiny—to draw out God's people from Egypt.

Isn't it amazing to see the powerful way in which God works to raise up partners in his plan to reclaim his world! How does this help you to understand what it means for a person's life to be in God's hands? What does it tell you about God's commitment to train and prepare his people to be partners in his plan?

2. In this first recorded act of Moses, with whom did he identify? (See Exodus 2:11 – 12.)

How do you think Moses learned to view the Hebrews as his own people and to choose suffering instead of the "good life" of Egyptian nobility?

Where do you think Moses got his passion to stand against injustice being imposed on the weak?

THINK ABOUT IT

It is difficult to know if God approved when Moses killed the Egyptian (by "striking" or "smiting" him, Exodus 2:11–12). The next place the same Hebrew word is used is when Moses strikes the rock (Numbers 20:11–12), and in this instance God is obviously displeased with Moses' action. Although God at times makes his ways known by "smiting," he more often exercises mercy and patience before he acts with power. For example, only after nine plagues did God act more destructively in the tenth plague and then drown the Egyptian army in the Red Sea.

RAMSES SMITING HIS ENEMIES BEFORE AMUN

Did Moses "strike" the Egyptian because he had been influenced by the "rod" of Pharaoh during the forty years he lived as a prince of Egypt? (Remember all of the carvings of Pharaoh with his raised rod, "smiting" his enemies?) Is it possible that Moses spent the next forty years as a shepherd in the desert because he needed comparable preparation for leading God's people like a shepherd?

3. Which other qualities of God do you think Moses demonstrated by his actions? (See Exodus 2:13 – 20.)

4. What do you notice about the compassion and character of God when he assigns to Moses the task of delivering his people from Egypt? (See Exodus 3:7 – 10.)

In what ways was Moses like God in his compassion, concern, and desire to bless others?

5. In addition to the godly quality of character that Moses demonstrated, how do we know that God thought highly of Moses? (See Exodus 33:17; Numbers 12:3 – 8; Deuteronomy 34:10 – 12; Hebrews 3:2, 5.)

6. Moses already had found favor with God, so why might God have wanted him to be a shepherd for forty years before leading the Hebrews out of Egypt? (See Psalm 23:1 – 3; 78:52 – 53; 80:1; 95:6 – 7; Isaiah 40:11.)

What does this extensive time of preparation say to you about the importance of the work to which God was calling Moses?

How much time and effort are we willing to put into preparation for the work to which God has called us, and does our commitment adequately reflect the importance of our work to God?

DID YOU KNOW?

Moses named one of his sons Gershom (Exodus 18:3), which likely comes from the Hebrew *ger sham*, which means "a stranger there." This may indicate Moses' deep awareness that God's people would not remain in Egypt, and that God would faithfully fulfill his covenant with Abraham. At the time his son was born, do you think Moses had any idea what part he had yet to play in fulfilling God's plan?

Faith Lesson (6 minutes)

No figure in the Hebrew Bible is more central than Moses, who is called "the servant of the Lord." In the Christian Testament, Moses is mentioned more often than any other Hebrew Bible figure, and these references emphasize parallels between the work of Moses and Jesus. Moses prefigured, prophesied, and prepared for the Messiah's coming. As servants of the Lord, both Moses and Jesus had a deep faith in God. They encountered opposition and wrestled with the burden of God's will, yet they obediently submitted to him and asked for God's mercy when others disobeyed God's commands.

1. In Numbers 12:6 – 8, God himself described Moses as "my servant" with whom he speaks "face to face."

   a. How would you like God to use such a title when speaking of you?

   b.   Do you think it is possible for that to happen? Why or why not?

2.   Because of his remarkable devotion as a servant of God, Moses is an example for followers of Jesus today.

   a.   What led to Moses being known by this special title?

   b.   How willing are you to learn what made Moses so special to God?

   c.   What level of intensity in your commitment and your daily actions do you think following Moses' example would require of you?

3.   When have you or someone you know realized that God has been guiding and shaping you through your life experiences in order to prepare you for something you never imagined would happen?

What effect has that experience had on your understanding of how God works?

How has that experience shaped your response to the influences and opportunities that surround you today?

In what ways does that experience fuel a passionate commitment to obey God and to care for his people regardless of the sacrifices you may be required to make?

Closing (1 minute)

Together, read Joshua 22:5 aloud: "Be very careful to keep the commandment and the law that Moses the servant of the LORD gave you: to love the LORD your God, to walk in all his ways, to obey his commands, to hold fast to him and to serve him with all your heart and all your soul."

Then pray about what God has shown you about being a "servant of the Lord." Tell him that you want to be completely devoted to his service no matter what sacrifices you will have to make. Commit to obeying his commands and holding fast to him no matter what circumstances you face. Ask him to show you how to pass on your faith to other people as effectively as Moses' parents passed on their faith to their three children.

Memorize

Be very careful to keep the commandment and the law that Moses the servant of the LORD gave you: to love the LORD your God, to walk in all his ways, to obey his commands, to hold fast to him and to serve him with all your heart and all your soul.

Joshua 22:5

Tested and Trained to Be God's Message

In-Depth Personal Study Sessions

Day One | Commissioned to Be God's Servant

The Very Words of God

> *Now the cry of the Israelites has reached me, and I have seen the way the Egyptians are oppressing them. So now, go. I am sending you to Pharaoh to bring my people the Israelites out of Egypt. But Moses said to God, "Who am I, that I should go to Pharaoh and bring the Israelites out of Egypt?"*

Exodus 3:9–11

Bible Discovery

It's Too Big a Job, Lord!

For eighty years, God had been preparing Moses for the daunting task of confronting Pharaoh and his powerful dynasty in order to free the Hebrew slaves to worship their God in the desert. At last the promise God gave to Abraham centuries earlier would be fulfilled! But like many of us, Moses doubted his ability to carry out his mission in God's redemptive plan. Focused on his own human qualifications, Moses was not shy about giving God excuses.

1. In Scripture we can find numerous examples of God revealing himself to people and calling them to obey him for a specific task or mission. Read Genesis 22:11 – 18; 46:2 – 4; 1 Samuel 3:10 – 11; Luke 22:31 – 32; Acts 9:3 – 6. What insight do these historic revelations from God provide into how God called Moses (Exodus 3:4 – 10) and assigned a mission to this desert shepherd?

THINK ABOUT IT

A rabbinic *midrash* (teaching) suggests that when God started explaining what he wanted Moses to do, the Torah recorded only part of the conversation—God's response to what Moses was thinking. Whether or not this is true, we can imagine how the conversation might have gone:

The Lord: I have indeed seen the misery of my people in Egypt. (Exodus 3:7)

Moses: Yes! Wonderful.

The Lord: I have heard them crying out because of their slave drivers, and I am concerned about their suffering. (3:7)

Moses: They will be so grateful!

The Lord: So I have come down to rescue them from the hand of the Egyptians and to bring them up out of that land into a good and spacious land, a land flowing with milk and honey. (3:8)

Moses: It's about time. They have been slaves for years! Since before I was born!

The Lord: So now, go. I am sending you to Pharaoh to bring my people the Israelites out of Egypt. (3:10)

Moses: Whoa! Me? Just a minute!

Obviously this conversation is not in the Scripture, but thinking of it in this way helps us to comprehend Moses' joyous reaction when God declared his love and compassion for his suffering people. It also helps us to feel the crisis Moses experienced when God declared that Moses was his chosen messenger to Pharaoh!

2. When God first identified himself, Moses initially hid his face out of fear. But when God revealed his concern for the Hebrews and designated Moses to be his instrument for confronting Pharaoh and leading God's people out of Egypt, Moses suddenly found his voice. He began insisting to the Creator of the universe that he was not capable of the assignment! Consider Moses' example of honesty with God as he struggled with a sense of his own inadequacy and uncertainty. (See Exodus 3:7 – 4:17.)

a. What was Moses' first excuse for why he was unable to
    fulfill God's commission? (See Exodus 3:11 – 12.)

b. Was he doubting himself or God?

c. What would make Moses adequate for the task, and what
    did God promise Moses as a personal sign of his pres-
    ence?

d. What do you think was behind Moses' second objection
    to God's commission — doubt about himself or doubt
    about God? (See Exodus 3:13 – 22.)

e. What insight do you gain from God's answer regarding
    the spiritual state of the Hebrews? Might they have some
    questions about their God? Why or why not?

f. What is the common insecurity in Moses' third and
    fourth excuses? (See Exodus 4:1 – 17.)

g. In what ways are God's responses to all of Moses' excuses similar? (Write down God's answer to each of Moses' four excuses.)

h. Despite his excellent qualifications, on whom did Moses need to depend in order to successfully carry out this mission?

3. What valuable insight do you think God's people today can gain from Moses' struggle with inadequacy to accomplish God's calling?

THINK ABOUT IT
Qualified for What?

In one sense, Moses appears to be well qualified for the mission to which God assigned him. He had lived in Pharaoh's palace for nearly forty years, so he knew Egyptian life and culture. He spoke the language, knew many high ranking officials (some of whom were probably still alive), was familiar with the protocol of Pharaoh's court, and understood Egyptian religious beliefs. As a Hebrew, he knew his own roots as well. And having spent forty years as a shepherd in the very desert through which God wanted him to lead Israel to the Promised Land, he knew the best routes on which to travel, where to find springs and wells, the best grazing areas, and where other people typically lived.

Despite how well prepared Moses was, God emphasized that Moses could be confident of success because *he* would go with him to help him! Do you

continued on next page . . .

think God might have wanted Moses to remember that even when God leads us through experiences that qualify us for a particular task, we can accomplish nothing except as God's power enables us? Might there be a danger in depending on our own qualifications to accomplish God's work? How would you describe the way in which God applies his wisdom, power, and strength to the qualifications, passion, and commitment of his human partners in order to accomplish his plan of redemption?

4. Read Exodus 4:10, Isaiah 6:1 – 7, and Jeremiah 1:4 – 7. Notice the similarities between Moses' response to God and the responses of Isaiah and Jeremiah. Why do you think an assignment to speak God's words would inspire a response of unworthiness?

POINT TO PONDER

Scholars are not sure whether Moses' fourth excuse, of being "slow of speech and tongue" (Exodus 4:10; literal Hebrew: "uncircumcised lips"), indicates a speech impediment or fear that after forty years away from Egyptians and Hebrews he would not be fluent in languages or have necessary public speaking skills.

In either instance, why might God choose someone with a speech deficiency to be his spokesperson to the world? What did he teach Moses, the Hebrews, and us by using Moses as his mouthpiece? How might Paul's message to the Corinthian followers of Jesus (1 Corinthians 1:18 – 31) be similar to the lesson Moses had to learn when he was called by God?

Reflection

We might find it easy to criticize Moses for all of his excuses, yet he showed great boldness during his personal encounter with Almighty God. We also often respond to God's call on our lives with excuses. So we have much to learn from the interaction between God and Moses regarding God's plan and how he and Moses would accomplish it.

What kinds of people does God call to ministry and leadership?

What might be the advantages and disadvantages of God calling a competent and experienced person to fulfill his work?

What might be the advantages and disadvantages of God calling an inexperienced person to fulfill his work?

What do you think qualifies a person to fulfill God's mission? Godly parents? Career success? Faithful obedience? Or something else?

When God calls you to a task that you cannot see yourself capable of accomplishing, how do you feel, and how do you respond to him?

Do you ever think you are qualified to accomplish the work God has given you? Why or why not?

What are the dangers of feeling adequate to handle whatever God has given you to do?

What might God want you to learn — about yourself, about him — through situations that require more than you feel you have to give?

People today can hear God speak through the testimony of his Word, the Bible. If you lack confidence in your capability to accomplish what God has set before you, or if you lack confidence in God's faithfulness to go with you into unknown territory, consider what God's Word says:

What is the only way to have confidence in being the person God calls you to be? (See 1 John 2:5 - 6.)

What is the only way to have confidence in fulfilling the mission God has called you to accomplish? (See Deuteronomy 1:29 - 33; Psalm 9:10.)

Memorize

Moses said to God, "Who am I, that I should go to Pharaoh and bring the Israelites out of Egypt?"
And God said, "I will be with you."

Exodus 3:11 - 12

Day Two | In the Footsteps of Moses

The Very Words of God

> *I will raise up for them a prophet like you from among their brothers;*
> *I will put my words in his mouth, and he will tell them everything I*
> *command him. If anyone does not listen to my words that the prophet*
> *speaks in my name, I myself will call him to account.*

Deuteronomy 18:18 – 19

Bible Discovery

Elijah and Jesus: Following in Moses' Example

Moses was a great prophet and leader of God's people, but more than that he had a remarkable face-to-face and heart-to-heart relationship with God. If we look at the two greatest prophets who came after Moses — Elijah and Jesus (and Jesus was both prophet and Redeemer) — we see parallels to Moses in their experiences, character, mission, and relationship with God. What insights can we gain from their lives that will help us to walk faithfully with God?

1.   Moses and Elijah appeared at crucial points in the spiritual and political history of God's people. They both interceded for God's people, asking him to remain faithful to his covenant despite their disobedience. Through Moses, God rescued Israel from the bondage of slavery and idolatry in Egypt and shaped his people through the giving of the Torah and during their desert wanderings. Through Elijah, God called his people out of pagan worship to faithfulness and preserved a remnant of them who faithfully lived by his commands. As they carried out their respective roles, Moses and Elijah shared an amazing number of similar experiences for us to consider. (And those listed below are only some of them!)

Text	Moses' Experience	Elijah's Experience
Ex. 2:15; 1 Kings 19:1 – 3		

continued on next page . . .

Text	Moses' Experience	Elijah's Experience
Ex. 2:15–22; 1 Kings 17:7–9		
Ex. 3:1; 19:1; 24:15; 33:21–23; 1 Kings 19:1–9, 12–13		
Ex. 16:8, 12; 1 Kings 17:6		
Num. 11:11–12; 1 Kings 17:19–21		
Ex. 3:1–4, 10; 5:1; 7:10; 9:1; 1 Kings 17:1; 18:1–2		
Ex. 24:4; 1 Kings 18:30		
Ex. 32:11–14; 1 Kings 18:36–37		
Exodus 32:25–29; 1 Kings 18:37–40		
Exodus 3:6; 33:21–22; 34:2; 1 Kings 19:11–13		
Deut. 34:1–6; 2 Kings 2:1–18		

2. Although every godly prophet was in a sense similar to Moses, the ancient Jewish people believed the coming prophet God promised to send would be the Messiah. (See Deuteronomy 18:17 - 19.)

a. In what ways did Moses "picture" what the Messiah would be like, and how did Jesus present himself in relationship to Moses? (See John 3:14 – 15; 5:46.)

b. For what reasons did some people believe that Jesus was *the* prophet? (See John 6:14; 7:37 – 40.)

c. Although Jesus was like Moses, how did the writer of Hebrews describe their differences? (See Hebrews 3:1 – 6.)

3. Moses, Elijah, and Jesus shared common experiences that were rooted in their intimate relationship with and obedience to God.

a. Read Exodus 34:1 – 2, 27 – 28. How long was Moses with God on the mountain? What did Moses do (and not do) during that time? On what did Moses focus his attention during that time? What do you think he learned about trusting and depending on God during that time?

b. Read 1 Kings 19:1 – 9. How long did it take Elijah to travel from Beersheba to the mountain of God? What sustained him during that time? (Apparently Elijah, like Moses, did not eat or drink during that time.) What do you think was taking place in Elijah's relationship with God during that time?

c. Read Matthew 4:1 – 11; Mark 1:12 – 13; Luke 4:1 – 13. How long was Jesus in the desert? During that time, what did he live without and how was he sustained? Given the fact that Satan was tempting him then, on what do you think Jesus was focusing his attention?

4. God worked in powerful ways through Moses, Elijah, and Jesus. He used them to reveal his power through awesome miracles. But even more amazing was the way he furthered his plan of redemption through their faithful obedience to his calling. Sadly, not everyone who witnessed the power of God at work through these men recognized God's purpose and responded as God desired.

a. As you read the following portions of the Scripture, take note of how people responded to God's great acts and the impact those miracles appear to have had on the way people responded to the next "crisis" that came along — whether in their relationship with God and/or their response to circumstances.

Text	The Miracle(s) and What It Accomplished	The People's Apparent Response to Miracle(s)	The People's Response to the Next "Crisis"
Moses: Ex. 14:21 – 31; 15:1 – 18, 22 – 24			

Text	The Miracle(s) and What It Accomplished	The People's Apparent Response to Miracle(s)	The People's Response to the Next "Crisis"
Moses: Ex. 19:1–7, 16–19; 24:15–18; 32:1–6			
Elijah: 1 Kings 18:22–40; 19:1–4, 18			
Jesus: Mark 8:1–21			

b. What did you realize from these examples about:

how difficult it is to change the hearts of people?

how quickly people tend to forget what God has done for them?

Reflection

As this brief exploration of Moses, Elijah, and Jesus illustrates, Scripture is rich with insights that teach, inspire, and guide us. But how much do we really internalize these Bible examples (as well as contemporary experiences) to ensure that we maintain a sense of the awe and wonder of God's presence and power?

What is your response when you realize that despite God's great miracles in the past, his people so quickly turned their backs on him or ignored his calling?

To what extent do you respond in similar ways to the mighty work God does in your life, or the work you witness in the life of another person?

Even when we desire to love the Lord our God with all our heart, all our soul, and all our strength, it is not easy to keep a sense of vibrant freshness in our relationship with God. When I (Ray) faced coronary bypass surgery several years ago, it was quite traumatic. But God brought me through the unknown and the risks. As I recuperated, God's presence was intensely real and intimately near to me. Although I remain deeply aware of and grateful for God's gift of renewed health, I feel saddened by how much my intimate sense of God's grace and presence has faded and by how often I forget to trust him.

In what ways do you relate to this sense of loss in your relationship with God?

Why do you think our experiences of God's power and amazing love tend to fade away?

What can we do to sustain the joy and enthusiasm of an intimate encounter with God after experiencing him in a powerful way?

In what ways do you desire to follow the example of Moses, Elijah, and Jesus as you live out your commitment to obey God and live in such a way that other people will come to know him?

In which of their footsteps are you willing to walk?

Day Three | The Commitment of Elijah

The Very Words of God

> And the word of the LORD came to him: "What are you doing here, Elijah?"
>
> He replied, "I have been very zealous for the LORD God Almighty. The Israelites have rejected your covenant, broken down your altars, and put your prophets to death with the sword. I am the only one left, and now they are trying to kill me too."

> *1 Kings 19:9 – 10*

Bible Discovery

Filled with the Fire of the Lord

Elijah, like Moses, demonstrated great passion for God and expended great physical and spiritual effort in order to lead God's people into a life of faithful obedience to God. Like Moses, Elijah climbed mountains, confronted kings, and crossed deserts. He saw God work in mighty ways and sought to know God as one would an intimate friend. Elijah remains the picture of an impassioned servant of God — the model of a person who served God wholeheartedly. By studying his life and discovering the depth of his commitments, perhaps we will cultivate a deeper passion for obeying and experiencing God in our lives.

1. One of the qualities that demonstrated Elijah's fire for the Lord was his bold obedience to do whatever God commanded. When God gave Elijah a message to tell the king, what was taking place in Israel? (See 1 Kings 16:29 – 33; 17:1 – 3.)

What was God's message, and how well do you think it was received? Why?

2. When the allotted time was up, God gave Elijah another message to deliver. What risk(s) did Elijah face by obeying God's command? (See 1 Kings 18:1 – 24.)

In what ways did Elijah demonstrate a fearless trust in God as he carried out God's command?

What was Elijah's spiritual concern for the people?

3. The confrontation Elijah arranged between himself (as the prophet of the Lord) and the prophets of Baal was no easy task. As you continue exploring this confrontation, write down the type of maximum effort Elijah expended in order to serve God faithfully and guide Israel back to God.

The Text	Physical/Spiritual/Emotional Effort Elijah Expended
1 Kings 18:20–29	What did Elijah do while the prophets of Baal were praying?
1 Kings 18:30–35	How much effort does it take to build a stone altar big enough for a bull and to dig a trench around it? How much work is it for one person to slaughter a bull and cut it into pieces?
1 Kings 18:40	How much work is it to capture 850 people, move them down a mountain, and kill them?

The Text	Physical/Spiritual/Emotional Effort Elijah Expended
1 Kings 18:41–46	How many more times did Elijah climb the mountain, and then what did he do?
1 Kings 19:1–9	How much effort did it take to run from Jezreel (north of Jerusalem) to Beersheba, then travel another day into the desert, then go to Mount Horeb?

Can you think of anyone other than Elijah who has expended this much effort to obey God?

How does Elijah's commitment and effort influence you to evaluate the effort you put into your walk with God?

DID YOU KNOW?

No one knows exactly where the 1 Kings 18 events occurred on Mount Carmel, so we don't know exactly how far it was from the altar site to the Kishon Valley. But the distance would be at least two miles and more than a thousand-foot climb.

At its closest point, the distance from Mount Carmel to the ruins of Jezreel is 18.6 miles (with an elevation change of more than 1,000 feet)! The distance between Jezreel and Beersheba (1 Kings 19:1–5) is about 120 miles. Elijah then went to Mount Horeb, which, if it is the traditional Mount Sinai, is more than 190 miles away. If Mount Horeb is one of the alternative sites, the distance may have been much farther—across some of the most forbidding mountainous desert in the world.

4. Elijah was utterly exhausted after the events on Mount Carmel and Jezebel's threat on his life (1 Kings 19:1 – 4). Even so, he walked nearly two hundred additional miles before reaching Mount Horeb, where God met with him. (See 1 Kings 19:9 – 18.)

    a. How satisfying do you think Elijah's meeting with God was?

    b. In what ways was Elijah's meeting with God similar to Moses' meeting with God on the same mountain?

    c. What assignments did God give to Elijah, and what hope did God provide to show that his plan for redemption had not failed?

Reflection

Because Elijah passionately and obediently served God, God accomplished much through him. When Elijah's days on earth were fulfilled, God designated Elisha to succeed him. What kind of a prophet would Elisha be? For starters, he wanted a "double portion" of Elijah's spirit even though Elijah had warned him that he was asking for a difficult thing (2 Kings 2:9 – 12)!

Would you want to have a "double portion" of Elijah's spirit? Why or why not?

We may tend to think that Elijah's passion and the extraordinary effort he put into obeying God is beyond our reach. But James reminds us that "Elijah was a man just like us" (James 5:17 – 18).

Do you think God still requires his followers to give him maximum effort — even when all the results are due to God acting through his servants? Why or why not?

How much effort do you think it takes to serve the Lord?

What do you think would be required of you — spiritually, physically, emotionally, intellectually — and how far would you be willing to push yourself to give maximum effort to obeying the Lord?

When Jesus lived on earth, he was mistaken for Elijah. How much risk is there that your walk with God is so zealous and so closely follows that of Jesus that someone would mistake you for Elijah?

How might you want that perception to change, and what effort are you willing to expend to become more zealous and more like Jesus?

Memorize

> Do not let your heart envy sinners,
>   but always be zealous for the fear of the Lord.
> There is surely a future hope for you,
>   and your hope will not be cut off.

Proverbs 23:17–18

DATA FILE

The Broom Tree

Broom trees, *rotem* in Hebrew, are common in the wadis (flood canyons) of the desert. Although we might think of them more as shrubs, broom trees are the shade trees of the desert. They provide a small area of shade — just enough for some relief from the intense heat.

A BROOM TREE PROVIDES "JUST ENOUGH" SHADE TO MAKE THE DESERT HEAT TOLERABLE ENOUGH TO CONTINUE ON.

When Elijah was running for his life, he sat under a broom tree and asked God to end his life. Instead, God sent an angel to provide food, water, and rest so that Elijah could continue on toward his meeting with God at Mount Horeb.

Life in the desert is difficult, and sometimes painful, but the Scripture describes God as our shade (Psalm 121:5–6). God may not make the pain and difficulty go away, but he will provide enough shade to go another hour, another day, another week. He will provide "just enough" to keep his people dependent on him.

Day Four | Meeting God on His Mountain

The Very Words of God

> And the Lord said, "I will cause all my goodness to pass in front of you. … But," he said, "you cannot see my face, for no one may see me and live." Then the Lord said, "There is a place near me where you may stand on a rock. When my glory passes by, I will put you in a cleft in the rock and cover you with my hand until I have passed by. Then I will remove my hand and you will see my back; but my face must not be seen."

> *Exodus 33:19–23*

Bible Discovery

Knowing God Face to Face

It is a difficult thing — not a bad thing, but a difficult thing — to know God and to love him with all your heart, soul, and strength. Both Moses and Elijah had the passion and commitment to know and love God in this way. They knew that they would expend every bit of their strength and energy to obey God. And until the last day of their earthly lives, God expected amazing, obedient commitment from them. But God also rewarded them for their faithfulness when he allowed them to meet with him personally and get to know him face to face on Mount Sinai.

1. Knowing God as Moses knew him at times demanded hard, physical work. As you read the following accounts of Moses' trips up Mount Sinai, think about the tremendous commitment that this eighty-year-old man demonstrated to God by

climbing up and down Mount Sinai (whichever mountain it actually is). Consider the effort Moses was expending to obey God and the gift of strength he was receiving from God to accomplish the task. What do you think was happening in the relationship between Moses and God during this time?

The Text	The Effort to Obey God/The Reward of Getting to Know Him
Ex. 19:3–8	To receive God's message for Israel
Ex. 19:8–14	To deliver Israel's answer
Ex. 19:20	To receive instructions
Ex. 19:24–25	To get Aaron
Ex. 20:18–21	To approach God in the thick darkness
Ex. 24:1–11	With the elders of Israel to make the covenant with God
Ex. 24:12–18	To receive the two tablets of the covenant
Ex. 34:1–4, 27–29	Carried up two stone tablets on which to write the words of the covenant

2. On his last day on earth, God asked Moses to climb Mount Nebo near the Dead Sea. This climb would have been at least twelve miles with an elevation gain of 3,500 feet. How old was Moses, and what resistance or hesitation did he have toward another all-out climb to meet with God? (See Deuteronomy 34:1 - 12.)

3. After the golden calf incident, Moses told the Hebrews, "Perhaps I can make atonement for your sin." As a mediator between Israel and God, he went back up the mountain and asked God to forgive their sin. (See Exodus 32:7 - 14, 30 - 35.)

    a.   How hard did Moses work, and what was he willing to sacrifice in order to persuade God to change his mind and forgive the Israelites? (See Exodus 32:11 – 14, 31 – 32.)

    b.   How are Moses and Jesus alike and different in their work as mediators? (See Hebrews 3:1 – 6; 4:15.)

4.   The reward for Moses' faithfulness and extraordinary effort to obey every command of God was an intimate relationship with him that very few people have experienced. Although Moses could not see God face to face, Scripture says that God spoke with Moses "face to face" like the closest of friends. (See Exodus 33:7 – 23; John 17.)

    a.   How honestly did Moses talk with God, and in what ways do their conversations remind you of Jesus' conversations with his Father?

    b.   In what ways were the concerns Moses shared with God for the people God had entrusted to his care similar to the concerns Jesus expressed to his Father?

    c.   How did God respond when Moses asked to see his glory? When had Jesus seen the glory of God?

5. What characteristics of God did Moses see or hear when he met God in the cave and saw God's back and on the mountain when he heard God proclaim his character? (See Exodus 33:19 – 23; 34:6 – 7.) [HINT: Jewish tradition finds thirteen traits.]

Why do you think the God of such power, wisdom, glory, and holiness would want Moses' dominant impression of him to be of other aspects of his character?

In what way(s) do you think Moses' experience of seeing and hearing God benefited the Israelites as he led them for nearly forty more years?

DID YOU KNOW?

The Hebrew word translated "gentle whisper" in 1 Kings 19:12, *damamah*, implies "confidential speech," an intimate and gentle voice indicating trust. It is like the intimate words between a husband and his wife, or two close friends. Therefore the Creator's "gentle whisper" implies a trusting intimacy with someone he loves dearly.

6. When God revealed himself to Elijah on the mountain of God many years after he appeared to Moses, why do you think God did not appear in the wind, earthquake, or fire — as Elijah might have expected after what had just

happened on Mount Carmel? (See 1 Kings 18:22 – 24, 36 – 39; 19:7 – 14.)

Reflection

During his mountain meetings with Moses, God seems to have wanted Moses' first — and dominant — impression to be that of his loving, caring, patient, and forgiving character. The primary qualities God revealed to Moses and through him to the Israelites were love and gentle compassion. God also revealed to Elijah a gentle, loving, intimate side of his character. Although Jesus the Messiah did powerful miracles, he primarily taught through loving and compassionate acts rather than by thunder or fire. Even when he defeated sin, Jesus did so by choosing to sacrifice himself so that humankind might live. Today, divine love is still the primary way by which people are drawn to know (experience) God.

> In light of your view of what God is like, what surprised you as you considered the characteristics that he revealed through his relationships with Moses and Elijah and through his Son, Jesus?

> In what ways do you think *knowing* God (experiencing him through an intimate relationship) as opposed to *knowing about* God changes your understanding of who he is and how he wants to accomplish his plan of redemption?

> How might this influence your desire to live in such a way that other people will come to know who God is?

What changes might you need to make in order to reveal the intimate, caring, compassionate character of God through your life and your relationships with other people?

What do you feel when you ponder Moses' attempt to cover the Israelites' sin and realize that Jesus the Messiah did this for *you* — and all of humankind?

Moses pleaded with God to be merciful and to forgive the Israelites. What about Moses' heartfelt desires and obedient lifestyle enabled him to converse with God in this way?

Do you have the same intimate understanding of God's heart and the passion to plead for his mercy and forgiveness for those who do not know him? Why or why not?

As you interact with other people, and as they have the opportunity to see you interact with God, what do you think they are learning about him through the ways you think, speak, and act?

Day Five | Meeting with God on a Mountain

The Very Words of God

> *When Moses went up on the mountain, the cloud covered it, and the glory of the LORD settled on Mount Sinai. For six days the cloud covered the mountain, and on the seventh day the LORD called to Moses from within the cloud. To the Israelites the glory of the LORD looked like a consuming fire on top of the mountain. Then Moses entered the cloud as he went on up the mountain. And he stayed on the mountain forty days and forty nights.*

> *Exodus 24:15 – 18*

Bible Discovery

Understanding the Significance of the Transfiguration

Many parallels can be found between the lives of Moses and Jesus. But one significant similarity is seldom discussed — the fact that Moses and Jesus each climbed a mountain to meet with God. (And in Jesus' case, Moses and Elijah were there too!) This event is recorded in the gospels of Matthew, Mark, and Luke. As one of the most significant presentations of Jesus as the Messiah, this event is filled with images that have significant meaning in light of the events and text of the Hebrew Bible. So come, take a closer look at what happened when Moses went up to Mount Sinai and when Jesus was transfigured on the mountain.

1. Moses was God's prophet for the people of the exodus, but who fulfilled God's promise to send another prophet like Moses? (See Deuteronomy 18:15 – 19; John 6:14; 7:40; Acts 3:17 – 23.)

    According to God's promise, what were God's people to do when he sent another prophet like Moses?

2. After reading Exodus 24:15 – 25:9, Matthew 17:1 – 13, Mark 9:2 – 13, and Luke 9:28 – 36, complete the following comparison.

	Moses on a Mountain	Jesus on a Mountain
Number of accompanying "disciples"		
Where each story happened		
When God spoke to Moses; when God spoke after Jesus went up		
What God did after his glory appeared		
What covered them on the mountain		
What the glory of God did to the faces of Moses and Jesus		
Their relationship to "exodus" or leaving		
Event related to the "tabernacle"		

NOTE: The "tabernacle" link is quite subtle. In the Hebrew, the Exodus account says God's glory "settled" (*shakan*) on Mount Sinai. In the Mark and Luke accounts, the disciples wanted to build *mishkan*, which is translated in English as "shelters," "tabernacles," or "booths." *Shakan* is the root of *mishkan*, which links the two events.

Did you have any idea that these amazing parallels existed? Why do you think God unfolded his revelation in this manner?

What significant knowledge (experience) of God do you think Christians today are missing out on because we generally know so little about the Hebrew Bible and the role it played in the life and ministry of Jesus?

3. Matthew 17:1 – 5 and Deuteronomy 18:14 – 19 are linked together by the events that took place at the transfiguration. Consider:

   a. What did God promise to Israel?

   b. Why did Israel need a prophet, and what command did God give his people regarding the prophet who would come?

   c. What command did the voice give during the transfiguration regarding Jesus?

   d. What did that command mean in light of the promise mentioned in Deuteronomy?

4. Peter was quite impressed by the transfiguration when it happened (Matthew 17:4), and in time he came to understand its significance. What did Peter experience during

this event, and how did he use it to further God's plan of redemption? (See 2 Peter 1:16–21.)

What effect must his testimony have had on his audience?

What would the testimony that Jesus' disciples actually heard the voice of God have meant to Jewish people who knew that when Moses went up to Mount Sinai, Israel had been afraid to hear the voice of God?

Reflection

Moses and Elijah are significant in the Christian text, demanding to be heard and imitated in their passion for God, his people, and the mission of his people to be a "light to the Gentiles." Both prophets point clearly in conduct, passion, and mission to the greater figure, Jesus the Messiah, and his messianic work. Their example of living so that all the world would come to know God was widely recognized among the Jewish people. Therefore, for Moses and Elijah to play a significant role in the messianic imagery of the Christian text was a powerful testimony to Jesus' Jewish disciples and audience.

These faithful servants of God also are significant because God has only one story — one plan — to restore shalom to a world broken by sin. Hence all of God's people — Moses, Elijah, Jesus, and us — have a role in the story that is centered on the person and work of Jesus. Our Christian faith is deeply rooted in the history of the Jewish people and in God's redemptive plan.

Take a few moments to review and write down what you have learned during these six study sessions about God from those who met him "on the mountain."

Consider Moses' powerful walk of faith and obedience as he learned how God's gentleness, mercy, and love transform a people. In what ways do you want to have the kind of faith that Moses had?

How will you nurture your relationship with God so that you learn to trust and depend on him as you serve him?

Consider the strength and passion of Elijah and his longing for God's people to turn away from their idols and seek the God of their fathers. In what ways do you want to see people come to know (experience) the living God?

How much effort will you expend because you are zealous for the Lord?

Consider how Jesus — the Son of God — knew God intimately from beyond eternity and during his time on earth demonstrated the character of God in gentleness, mercy, and love — even to the point of giving his life for the redemption of humankind. How important is it to you that you know (experience) Jesus and listen (obey) to what he says?

Jesus, who knew God as no one else can, also knew the Hebrew Bible, and he lived his life by it. What does his example say to you about the importance of "listening" to the Word of God — Hebrew as well as Christian — and committing yourself to obeying it?

Memorize

A bright cloud enveloped them, and a voice from the cloud said, "This is my Son, whom I love; with him I am well pleased. Listen to him!"

Matthew 17:5

NOTES

Introduction

1. Jesus' death (as the Lamb of God) was apparently on Passover; he was buried as the Unleavened Bread festival began, and was raised at the beginning of First Fruit.

2. Since I hold the Bible to be God's revealed word, I reject the arguments of many scholars who do not believe the exodus occurred or at least did not occur as the Bible describes it.

3. A defense of this position can be found in *The Moody Atlas of Bible Lands* by Barry J. Beitzel (Chicago: Moody Press, 1985).

4. A defense of this position can be found in *Exploring Exodus: The Origins of Biblical Israel* by Nahum M. Sarna (New York: Schocken Books, 1996).

Session One

1. Two suggestions as a beginning point are James K. Hoffmeier's *Ancient Israel in Sinai* (Oxford, England: Oxford Press, 2005), and Barry J. Beitzel's *The Moody Atlas of Bible Lands* (Chicago: Moody Press, 1985). Each of these authors presents the alternatives with their support taking the biblical text as a historically accurate source. They have a point of view — both support something close to the traditional location — but present evidence for other points of view as well. Their bibliographic references would provide a starting point to consider all major theories.

Session Two

1. I am indebted to Terence E. Fretheim for these ideas that are presented in his volume *Exodus: Interpretation, a Bible Commentary of Teaching and Preaching* (Louisville: John Knox Press, 1991).

2. Terence Fretheim has labeled this faith walk a "discipline of dailyness." *Exodus: Interpretation, a Bible Commentary of Teaching and Preaching*, 186.

Session Three

1. Sarna, Nahum, *JPS Torah Commentary: Exodus* (New York: Jewish Publication Society, 1991), 15.

2. See Genesis 25:13 – 16. Ishmael (son of Abraham and Hagar) had twelve sons who became the fathers of the twelve tribes of Ishmael. So Israel, the Ishmaelites, and the Edomites began with "twelve" leaders. Jesus followed the pattern with his disciples.

3. Telushkin, Rabbi Joseph, *The Book of Jewish Values* (New York: Bell Tower Publishers, 2000), 70.

4. The tribal arrangements are not mentioned until after the giving of the Ten Commandments, more than a year after the Amalekite attack. While the Hebrews may not have been carefully organized, Jewish thought maintains that the order of the tribes may precede the accounting in Numbers 25. If God organized the Hebrews later, then Dan was given the responsibility of protecting the weak after the attack or maybe because of it. They would then share the guilt of not protecting the weak in the rear from the Amalekites.

5. For a more complete treatment of "remembering" as an obligation on God's people, see *Exploring Exodus*, Nahum Sarna, 125.

Session Four

1. Notice that in both cases the number is rounded off. The Hebrew mind would see this as deliberate, in order to see the connection. That is the logic behind thinking that the Ten Commandments were given "around" Pentecost so they would be connected to that holiday and its meaning.

2. Credit is due Dwight Pryor for these distinctions, which I heard at an unpublished lecture in April 2002. For further development of the theme of the kingdom of heaven, I highly recommend his book *Unveiling the Kingdom of Heaven* (Dayton, Ohio: Center for Judaic Christian Studies, 2008; www.jcstudies.com).

3. See Lois Tverberg with Bruce Okkema, *Listening to the Language of the Bible* (Holland, Mich.: En-Gedi Resource Center, 2004; www.egrc.net).

Session Five

1. I owe this insight to a devotional by Jonathon Sacks, the Chief Rabbi of England.

2. See En-Gedi Resource Center at www.egrc.net: "Director's Article," June 2003, and "Biblical Dress: Tassels," See also Jacob Milgrom's Excursus 38 on Tassels (Tsitsit), *JPS Torah Commentary: Numbers* (New York: Jewish Publication Society, 1990).

ACKNOWLEDGMENTS

The people of God set out on a journey, a journey from bondage to freedom, a journey to the Promised Land, a place flowing with milk and honey. A simple journey, really: leave Egypt and walk to the Promised Land. All they had to do was cross the Sinai Desert and they were there. It would not take long; it was only two hundred miles. But God had another route planned. During the forty years that journey took, the Hebrews, concerned about themselves as we all are, became a community — a people who would put the Creator of the universe on display for a broken world.

The production of this study series is also the work of a community of people. Many contributed of their time and their talent to make it possible. Recognizing the work of that unseen community is to me an important confirmation that we have learned the lessons God has been teaching his people for three thousand and more years. It takes a community. These are the people God has used to make this entire series possible.

The Prince Foundation:

The vision of Elsa and Ed Prince — that this project that began in 1993 would enable untold thousands of people around the world to walk in the footsteps of the people of God — has never waned. God continues to use Elsa's commitment to share God's story with our broken world.

Focus on the Family:

Clark Miller — senior vice president, family ministries
Robert Dubberley — vice president, content development
Paul Murphy — manager, video post production
Cami Heaps — associate product marketing manager
Anita Fuglaar — director, global licensing

Carol Eidson — assistant to business services director

Brandy Bruce — editor

That the World May Know:

Alison Elders, Lisa Fredricks — administrative assistants

Chris Hayden — research assistant. This series would not have been completed nor would it have the excellence of content it has without his outstanding research effort.

The Image Group and Grooters Productions:

Mark Tanis — executive producer

John Grooters — producer/director

Amanda Cooper — producer

Eric Schrotenboer — composer/associate producer

Mark Chamberblin, Adam Vardy, Jason Longo — cinematography

Dave Lassanke, Trevor Lee — motion graphics

Rob Perry — illustrator

Sarah Hogan, Judy Grooters — project coordinators

Ken Esmeir — on-line editor and colorist

Kevin Vanderhorst, Stephen Tanner, Vincent Boileau — post-production technical support

Mark Miller, Joel Newport — music mixers

Keith Hogan, Collin Patrick McMillan — camera assistants

Andrea Beckman, Rich Evenhouse, Scott Tanis, Kristen Mitchell — grips

Shawn Kamerman — production assistant

Marc Wellington — engineer

Juan Rodriguez, Paul Wesselink — production sound

Ed Van Poolen — art direction

Zondervan:

John Raymond — vice president and publisher, church engagement

Robin Phillips — project manager, church engagement

Mike Cook — marketing director, church engagement

T. J. Rathbun — director, audio/visual production

Tammy Johnson — art director

Ben Fetterley — book interior designer

Greg Clouse — developmental editor

Stephen and Amanda Sorenson — writers

BIBLIOGRAPHY

To learn more about the cultural and geographical background of the Bible, please consult the following resources.

Basser, Herbert W. "The Jewish Roots of the Transfiguration," *Bible Review*, June 1998, page 30.

Beale, G. K. "An Exegetical and Theological Consideration of the Hardening of Pharaoh's Heart in Exodus 4–14 and Romans 9." *Trinity Journal* 5 NS, 1984, pages 129–154.

Beitzel, Barry J. *The Moody Atlas of Bible Lands.* Chicago: Moody Press,1985.

Berlin, Adele, and Marc Zvi Brettler. *Jewish Study Bible.* Philadelphia: Jewish Publication Society and New York: Oxford University Press, 2004.

Bivin, David. *New Light on the Difficult Words of Jesus: Insights from His Jewish Context.* Holland, Mich.: En Gedi Resource Center, 2005. (www.egrc.net).

Bottero, Jean, Elana Cassin and Jean Vercoutter, eds. *The Near East: The Early Civilizations.* New York: Delacorte Press, 1967.

Davis, John J. *Moses and the Gods of Egypt: Studies in Exodus.* Grand Rapids, Mich.: Baker Book House, 1971.

Edersheim, Alfred. *The Temple: Its Ministry and Services as They Were at the Time of Jesus Christ.* London: James Clarke & Co., 1959.

_____. *The Life and Times of Jesus the Messiah.* Peabody, Mass.: Hendrickson Publishers, 1993.

Feiler, Bruce. *Walking the Bible: A Journey by Land through the Five Books of Moses.* New York: HarperCollins, 2002.

Fretheim, Terence E. *Exodus: Interpretation, A Bible Commentary for Teaching and Preaching.* Louisville: John Knox Press, 1991.

Friedman, Richard Elliot. *Commentary on the Torah.* San Francisco: Harper, 2001.

Ginzberg, Louis. *An Unknown Jewish Sect.* New York: Jewish Theological Seminary of America, 1976, chapter 6.

Hillers, Delbert R. *Covenant: The History of a Biblical Idea.* Baltimore: Johns Hopkins Press, 1969.

Hoffmeier, James K. *Ancient Israel in Sinai*. Oxford: Oxford University Press, 2005.

_____. *Israel in Egypt*. Oxford: Oxford University Press, 1996.

Kline, Meredith G. *Treaty of the Great King*. Grand Rapids: William B. Eerdmans, 1962.

Lesko, Barbara and Leonard. "Pharaoh's Workers." *Biblical Archaeology Review*. January/February 1999.

Lesko, Leonard H., ed. *Pharaoh's Workers*. Ithaca, N.Y.: Cornell University Press, 1994.

Levenson, Jon D. *Sinai and Zion: An Entry into the Jewish Bible*. San Francisco: Harper, 1985.

Levine, Baruch A. *The JPS Torah Commentary: Leviticus*. Philadelphia: Jewish Publication Society, 1991.

Milgrom, Jacob. *The JPS Torah Commentary: Numbers*. Philadelphia: Jewish Publication Society, 1991.

Peterson, Eugene. *Eat This Book*. Grand Rapids, Mich.: Eerdmans Publishing, 2006.

Pryor, Dwight. *Unveiling the Kingdom of Heaven*. Dayton, Ohio: Center for Judaic Christian Studies, 2008. (www.jcstudies.com).

Riskin, Shlomo. "Exodus Defines the Birth of a Nation." *Torah Lights, vol. 2*. New York: Urim Publications, 2006.

Sarna, Nahum. *The JPS Torah Commentary: Exodus*. Philadelphia: Jewish Publication Society, 1991.

_____. *The JPS Torah Commentary: Genesis*. Philadelphia: Jewish Publication Society, 1991.

_____. *Exploring Exodus: The Origins of Biblical Israel*. New York: Schocken Books, 1996.

Silverman, David P. *Ancient Egypt*. Oxford: Oxford University Press, 1997.

Spangler, Ann and Lois Tverberg. *Sitting at the Feet of Rabbi Jesus*. Grand Rapids, Mich.: Zondervan, 2009.

Telushkin, Rabbi Joseph. *The Book of Jewish Values*. New York: Bell Tower Publishers, 2000, page 70.

Tigay, Jeffrey H. *The JPS Torah Commentary: Deuteronomy*. Philadelphia: Jewish Publication Society, 1991.

Tverberg, Lois with Bruce Okkema. *Listening to the Language of the Bible*. Holland, Mich.: En-Gedi Resource Center, 2004. (www.egrc.net).

Watterson, Barbara. *Gods of Ancient Egypt*. London: Sutton Publishing, 1996.

Wilkinson, Richard H. *The Complete Gods and Goddesses of Ancient Egypt.* Hong Kong: Thames and Hudson, 2003.

_____. *The Complete Temples of Ancient Egypt.* Hong Kong: Thames and Hudson, 2000.

Zevit, Ziony. "Three Ways to Look at the Ten Plagues." *Bible Review,* June 1990.

WEBSITE RESOURCES

Related to the temple of Amun Re at Karnak, Egypt:

http://touregypt.net/featurestories/templeofamun.htm

Article by Jimmy Dunn (includes reference sources) provides an overview of the temple of Amun Re at Karnak.

www.touregypt.net/featurestories/karnak2.htm

Several articles by Jim Fox (which include reference sources) about the different parts of the temple of Amun Re.

www.eyelid.co.uk/karnakb.htm

Provides an interactive map of the temple with photos.

http://dlib.etc.ucla.edu/projects/Karnak

A very good source that includes timelines and digital representations of the Karnak temple complex from different angles and periods.

http://en.wikipedia.org/wiki/karnak

Overview of the Karnak temple complex and information about the precinct of Amun Re. (CAVEAT: Wikipedia allows ANYONE to contribute information. It should therefore be scrutinized against other reliable sources for accuracy.)

www.ancient-wisdom.co.uk/egyptkarnak.htm

General information about Karnak and pictures of the main temple complex.

www.bibleplaces.com/karnak.htm

Pictures and an overview of the Karnak temple complex and a list of related websites.

www.pbs.org/wgbh/nova/egypt/explore/karnakrams.html

Interesting site with 360-degree interactive cameras positioned inside the temple of Amun Re.

Related to the pyramids of Egypt:

www.guarduans.net/egypt/pyramids.btm

Extensive collection of websites dedicated to the pyramids of Egypt.

http://en.wikipedia.org/wiki/Egyptian_pyramids

General information on the history, symbolism, and locations of pyramids with further readings and external links. (CAVEAT: Wikipedia allows ANYONE to contribute information. It should therefore be scrutinized against other reliable sources for accuracy.)

www.pbs.org/wgbh/nova/pyramid

Website related to the NOVA documentary "This Old Pyramid." Useful information on construction of the pyramids and the attempt to reconstruct a pyramid.

www.bbc.co.uk/history/ancient/egyptians/great_pyramid_01.sbtml

Loaded with scholarly articles, interactive content, timelines, etc.

www.eyelid.co.uk/pyr-temp.btm

Information on pyramids and temples, including computer generated reconstructions, interactive ground maps, photos, paintings and drawings.

www.egyptologyonline.com/welcome.btm

Provides information, resources, and scholarly articles on a variety of topics related to Egyptology.

www.ancientegypt.co.uk/pyramids/bome.html

The British Museum educational website on ancient Egypt. Includes stories showing the building of the pyramids and interactive exploration of a pyramid.

www.nationalgeographic.com/pyramids/pyramids.html

Website related to National Geographic's documentary "Egypt: Secrets of the Ancient World." Includes interactive timelines of ancient Egypt and the pyramids.

www.bibleplaces.com/giza.btm

Pictures and brief information about the pyramids of Giza. Includes a list of related websites.

www.touregypt.net/featurestories/pyramids.btm

Features extensive scholarly articles about ancient Egypt and the pyramids.

More Great Resources
from Focus on the Family®

Volume 1: Promised Land

This volume focuses on the Old Testament—particularly on the nation of ancient Israel, God's purposes for His people, and why He placed them in the Promised Land.

Volume 2: Prophets & Kings

This volume looks into the life of Israel during Old Testament times to understand how the people struggled with the call of God to be a separate and holy nation.

Volume 3: Life & Ministry of the Messiah

This volume explores the life and teaching ministry of Jesus. Discover new insights about the greatest man who ever lived.

Volume 4: Death & Resurrection of the Messiah

Witness the passion of the Messiah as He resolutely sets His face toward Jerusalem to suffer and die for His bride. Discover the thrill the disciples felt when they learned of His resurrection and were later filled with the Holy Spirit.

Volume 5: Early Church

Capture the fire of the early church with the faith lessons in Vol. 5. See how the first Christians lived out their faith with a passion that literally changed the world.

Volume 6: In the Dust of the Rabbi

"Follow a rabbi, drink in his words and be covered with the dust of his feet," says the ancient Jewish proverb. Come discover how to follow Jesus as you walk with teacher and historian Ray Vander Laan through the breathtaking terrain of Israel and Turkey and explore what it really means to be a disciple.

More Great Resources
from Focus on the Family®

Volume 7: Walk as Jesus Walked

Journey to Israel where 12 disciples walked the walk their rabbi Jesus taught them. Examining the culture and the politics of the first century, Vander Laan opens up the Gospels as never before.

Volume 8: God Heard Their Cry

Just when it seemed that Pharaoh could not be defeated, God provided for His people in ways they never could have imagined. Join Ray in ancient Egypt for his latest study of God's faithfulness to the Israelites—and a promise that remains true today.

The True Easter Story: The Promise Kept

Biblical historian Ray Vander Laan re-examines the dramatic events of Easter in *The True Easter Story: The Promise Kept*. New footage filmed in Israel, combined with earlier lessons from the series, shows the death and resurrection of Jesus as a fulfillment of the promise God made to Abraham. Approximately 44 minutes. Includes a bonus faith lesson, "Lamb of God."

The True Christmas Story: Herod the Great, Jesus the King

Experience *The True Christmas Story: Herod the Great, Jesus the King*, filmed in Israel with expanded footage at the site of Herod's fortress. Biblical scholar Ray Vander Laan uses earlier lessons from the series to contrast the lives of Jesus and Herod, making the Christmas story even more meaningful. This 43-minute teaching includes a bonus faith lesson, "Living Water."

FOR MORE INFORMATION

 Online:
Go to FocusOnTheFamily.com
In Canada, go to FocusOnTheFamily.ca

 Phone:
Call toll-free: 800-A-FAMILY
In Canada, call toll-free: 800-661-9800

BD08XTTWMK

Share Your Thoughts

With the Author: Your comments will be forwarded to the author when you send them to *zauthor@zondervan.com*.

With Zondervan: Submit your review of this book by writing to *zreview@zondervan.com*.

Free Online Resources at
www.zondervan.com

Zondervan AuthorTracker: Be notified whenever your favorite authors publish new books, go on tour, or post an update about what's happening in their lives at www.zondervan.com/authortracker.

Daily Bible Verses and Devotions: Enrich your life with daily Bible verses or devotions that help you start every morning focused on God. Visit www.zondervan.com/newsletters.

Free Email Publications: Sign up for newsletters on Christian living, academic resources, church ministry, fiction, children's resources, and more. Visit www.zondervan.com/newsletters.

Zondervan Bible Search: Find and compare Bible passages in a variety of translations at www.zondervanbiblesearch.com.

Other Benefits: Register yourself to receive online benefits like coupons and special offers, or to participate in research.

ZONDERVAN®

ZONDERVAN.com/
AUTHORTRACKER
follow your favorite authors